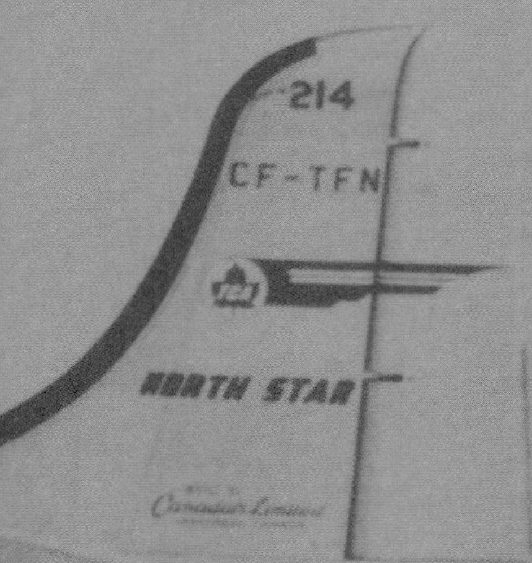
214
CF-TFN
NORTH STAR
AIR LINES

LEGENDS OF FLIGHT

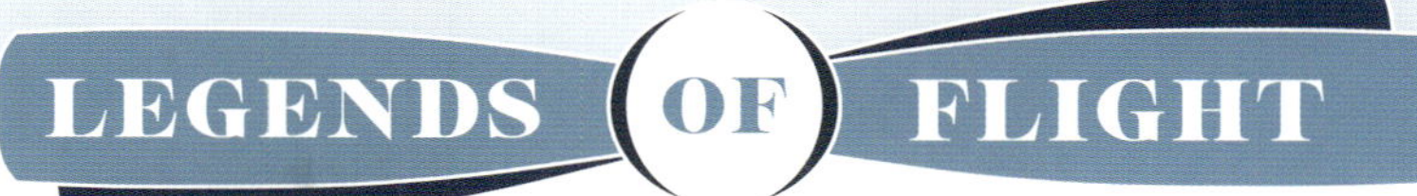

DOUGLAS DC-4, DC-6, AND DC-7

A Legends of Flight Illustrated History

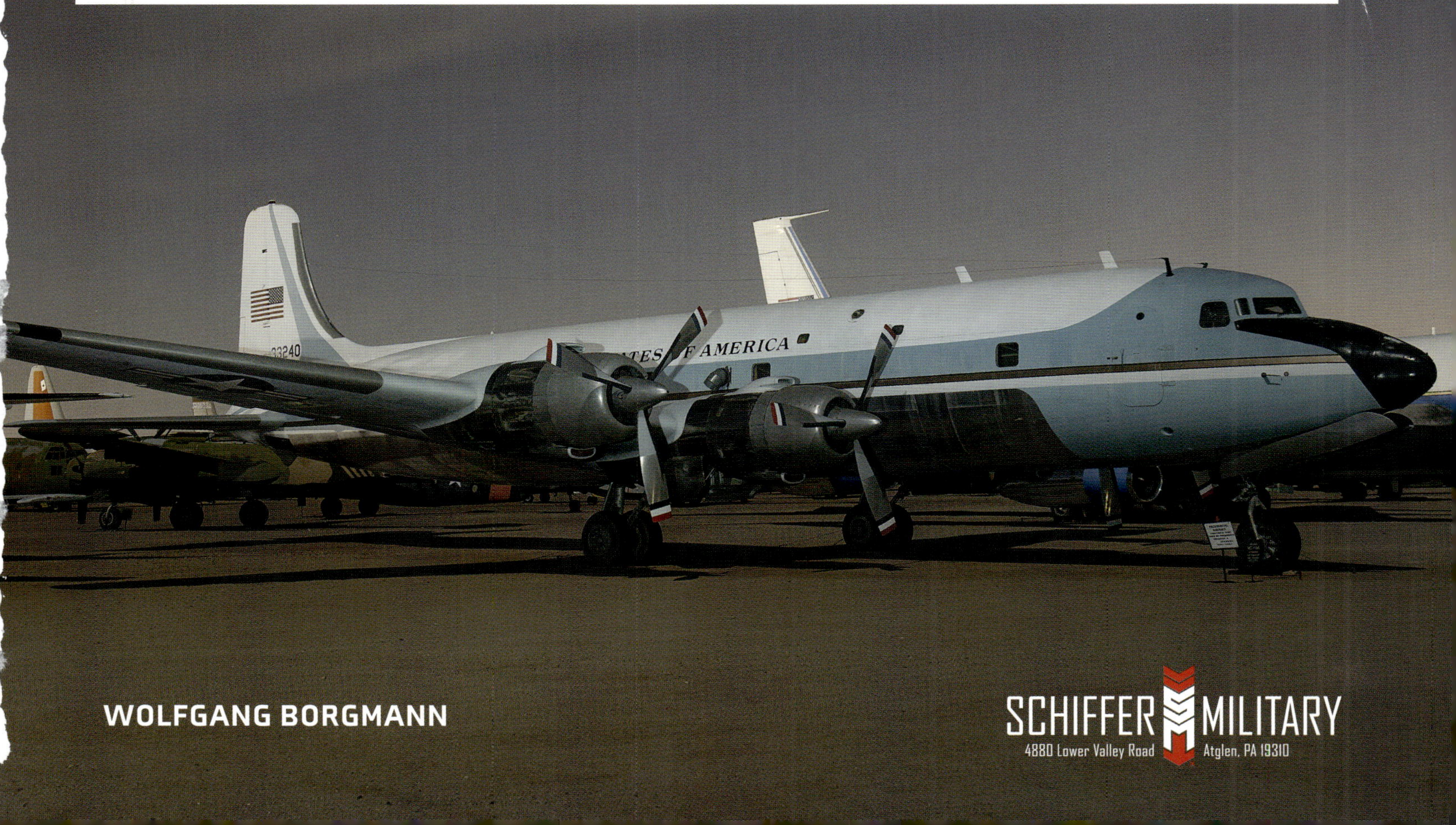

WOLFGANG BORGMANN

SCHIFFER MILITARY
4880 Lower Valley Road Atglen, PA 19310

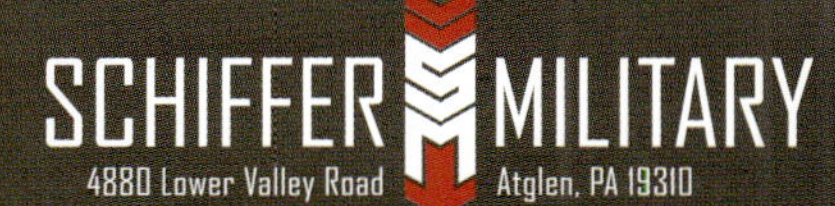

Other Schiffer books by the author
Airbus A300/310: A Legends of Flight Illustrated History,
    978-0-7643-6139-5
Boeing 737: A Legends of Flight Illustrated History,
    978-0-7643-6138-8

Other Schiffer books on related subjects
The Republic Airlines Story: An Illustrated History, 1945–1986,
    Terry Love, 978-0-7643-4247-9
Dornier Do X: The Story of Claude Dornier's Legendary Flying Boat,
    Volker A. Behr, 978-0-7643-4476-3

Translated from the German by David Johnston

Library of Congress Control Number: 2022948789

Designed by Justin Watkinson
Cover design by Molly Shields
Type set in DIN/Minion Pro

ISBN: 978-0-7643-6648-2
Printed in India

Published by Schiffer Publishing, Ltd.
4880 Lower Valley Road
Atglen, PA 19310
Phone: (610) 593-1777; Fax: (610) 593-2002
Email: Info@schifferbooks.com
Web: www.schifferbooks.com

For our complete selection of fine books on this and related subjects,
please visit our website at www.schifferbooks.com. You may also
write for a free catalog.

Schiffer Publishing's titles are available at special discounts for
bulk purchases for sales promotions or premiums. Special editions,
including personalized covers, corporate imprints, and excerpts, can
be created in large quantities for special needs. For more information,
contact the publisher.

We are always looking for people to write books on new and
related subjects. If you have an idea for a book, please contact
us at proposals@schifferbooks.com.

CONTENTS

FOREWORD

Following the exploration of scheduled air routes across the Artic, SAS passengers were greeted by the slogan: "First Over The Pole—Around The World" above the Douglas DC-6B and DC-7C entrance doors. *Courtesy of SAS Museum, Oslo*

DEPEND ON DOUGLAS!

This book describes the four-engine, propeller-driven Douglas Commercial (DC-) aircraft produced by the Douglas Aircraft Company, at one time the most important American producer of commercial aircraft. The story begins with the DC-4E Experimental, whose origins go back to plans from 1936, then continues with the DC-4A and DC-6 variants, before ending with the DC-7C, the last example of which was delivered to the Dutch airline KLM in December 1958. Those twenty-two years were a period of dramatic change in aircraft design. When the DC-4E—then the largest civil land-based aircraft in the world—took to the air for the first time on June 7, 1938, not even in his wildest dreams could any aircraft designer have imagined that within a few years, passengers would be flying between the continents at speeds nearing the speed of sound at altitudes of almost 40,000 feet. Spurred by the Second World War, the concurrent development of jet propulsion in Germany and Great Britain progressed so quickly that Douglas was able to produce the DC-8 four-engine jet airliner as the direct successor to the DC-7C Seven Seas.

PRESIDENTIAL
AIRCRAFT
(AIRFORCE ONE)
USED BY PRESIDENTS
KENNEDY &
JOHNSON
1961-1963
DOUGLAS
VC-118A
LIFTMASTER
VIP TRANSPORT

The Douglas DC-4's unique design made it possible for the Canadian aircraft maker Canadair to use it as the basis of development for its C-4 North Star and Argonaut, aircraft with a pressurized cabin and powered by four Rolls-Royce Merlin twelve-cylinder in-line engines. Also based on the Douglas DC-4, the ATL-98 Carvair had an unusual appearance reminiscent of the Boeing 747 Jumbo Jet, which appeared years later. This flying car and passenger ferry was produced by the British company Aviation Traders Ltd., part of the business empire of the man who would later be knighted as Sir Freddy Laker. In the 1950s, it was the fastest way for an automobile and its occupants to cross the English Channel between England and France. Chapters are dedicated to the North Star and Argonaut as well as to the Carvair.

The DC-4 "Clipper Stuttgart" served primarily on the Internal German Service (IGS) operated by Pan American World Airways between Berlin-Tempelhof and various airports in West Germany. Here it is seen after arriving at Hamburg airport. The Skymaster joined Pan American in 1946, with the registration N88901 and bore the names "Clipper Defiance" and "Clipper Hannover." It was retired in 1961. *Courtesy of Harald Borgmann*

The former DC-6 (VC-118A) Air Force One presidential aircraft against an impressive backdrop of an evening sky over Arizona on the museum grounds of the Pima Air and Space Museum. *Courtesy of John Bezosky, Pima Air and Space Museum*

The Douglas VC-118 "Independence" is one of ten former American presidential aircraft on display at the National Museum of the US Air Force. When this photo was taken, it was still in active service, operating as Air Force One when the sitting president was flying in the aircraft. *Courtesy of the US Air Force / Ken LaRock*

The first DC-4 operated by the Australian airline Quantas entered service on June 26, 1949. Its service premiere was on the newly opened route from Australia to Hong Kong. The Skymaster shown here was built in 1945 and remained in service with the airline, which was founded as Queensland & Northern Territory Aerial Services Ltd. on November 16, 1920, from 1949 until 1977. *Courtesy of Quantas*

QANTAS AIR CARGO
AUSTRALIA QANTAS
PACIFIC TRADER
ROYAL AIR MAIL
A

By the time Greenlandair put its two DC-6Bs in their colorful red-and-white livery into service, other airlines had long since been flying turboprops or jets. This DC-6B with the construction number 45329, the registration OY-DRC, and the name "Amalik" was built in 1957. It entered service with Greenlandair in 1971 and was photographed at Copenhagen-Kastrup airport on August 8, 1974—five years before it was retired. *Courtesy of Tom Weihe*

From the DC-4, Douglas developed two more large four-engine, propeller-driven airliners, the DC-6 Cloudmaster and the DC-7, which continued the success of their predecessor. The prototype of the Cloudmaster first flew on February 15, 1946, as the XC-112, and 704 examples of this type were built. It was followed by the DC-7, which took to the air for the first time on May 18, 1953. A total of 338 DC-7s were produced. It was this aircraft, together with the Lockheed L-1649A Starliner, that marked the worthy conclusion of the age of large propeller-driven airliners with piston engines on the world's long-haul routes. And, as with the DC-4E, American Airlines and Pan American World Airways were among the first customers to give the green light for the grand finale of the big Douglas propliners. It was the DC-6B and DC-7C Seven Seas whose proverbial Douglas reliability, in keeping with the company motto "Depend on Douglas," contributed to the opening of new trade routes between Europe, the West Coast of the US, and Japan in the 1950s, with regular polar air traffic over the Arctic. The background and special challenges of planning flight routes over the eternal ice, and the first transpolar passenger flights, are dealt with in a separate chapter of this work, which itself promises "high-proof" reading pleasure.

I hope that every reader enjoys the following flight into the "Golden Age of Aviation" aboard the Douglas Aircraft Company's large, four-engine DC propeller planes.

Wolfgang Borgmann
Oerlinghausen, winter 2022–23

Formed in 1963, the British airline Air Ferry operated DC-4s on passenger and freight flights. While on one of the latter, the aircraft shown here, with the registration G-ASOG, crashed on approach to Frankfurt/Main airport. Both pilots were killed. *Courtesy of Tom Weihe*

Sun-seeking tourists boarding a DC-7B of the Swedish airline Transair Sweden. The airline's origins go back to 1950. In 1975, it became a subsidiary of SAS, and in 1981 it ceased operations. The photo shows the DC-7B Sundsvall, registration SE-ERN, at Copenhagen on July 18, 1967. *Courtesy of Tom Weihe*

The cover of the SAS summer timetable from 1948 is decorated with three DC-4s, their tails painted in the colors of the nations that helped make up SAS—Denmark, Norway, and Sweden. *Courtesy of SAS / author's collection*

This photograph, taken at Stockholm-Bromma Airport, shows the handling equipment and the number of people, or trades, needed to transport a passenger (*front center*) on the Douglas DC-6B pictured. *Courtesy of the SAS Museum, Oslo*

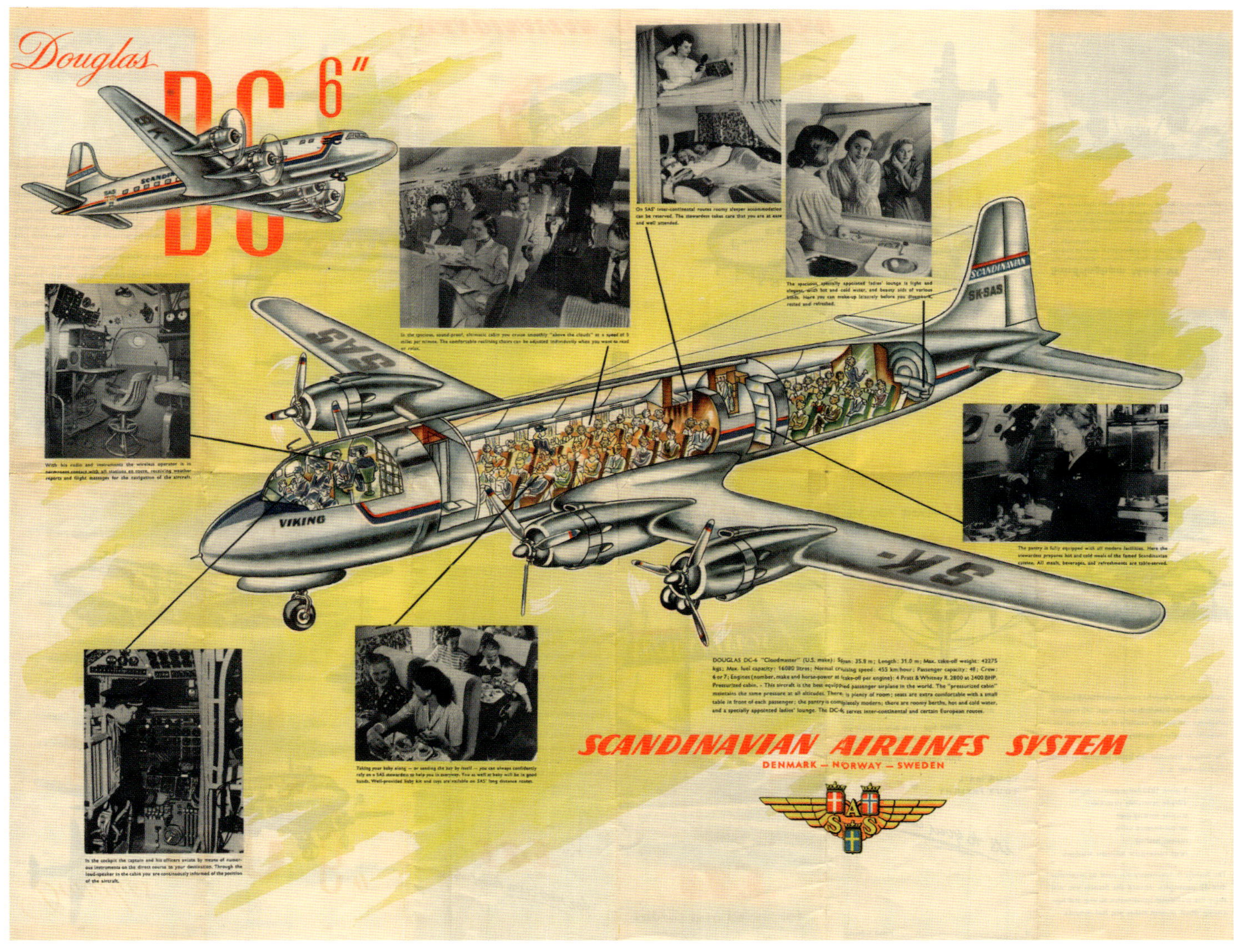

This cutaway drawing of an SAS DC-6 provides a view inside the cockpit and cabin of one of the Scandinavian Skymasters. *Courtesy of SAS / author's collection*

Standing in front of the former SAS headquarters at Stockholm-Bromma, a stewardess gazes longingly at the sky. Perhaps in anticipation of a flight on the DC-6 parked behind her? *Courtesy of SAS / author's collection*

In the so-called Golden Age of Air Transport, passengers were treated like royalty, like this gentleman dining in a four-poster bed against the backdrop of an SAS DC-6. SAS used this motif in various advertisements in the 1950s. *Courtesy of ABA/SAS Museum, Stockholm*

The in-flight service provided by the Swiss airline Swissair was legendary, including on its DC-6Bs. *Courtesy of Swissair / author's collection*

Not only passengers, but also valuable show horses were pampered on board Douglas propliners. Among them was this horse, unfortunately not known by name, which posed for the photographer shortly before its departure from Hamburg airport on a DC-4 freighter of Seaboard & Western Air. *Courtesy of Hans-Jürgen Kock*

Once boarded, the precious horse received VIP inflight-service. *Author's collection*

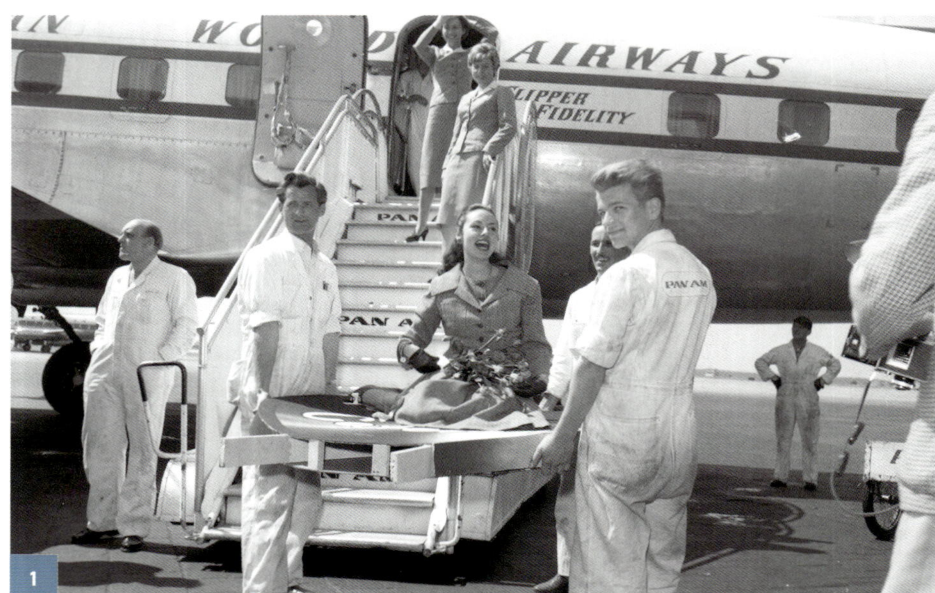

Los Angeles

SAS

Stars aboard Douglas four-engined propliners

1: Catharina Valente
2: Cary Grant
3: Ava Gardner
4: John Wayne
5: Josephine Baker
6: Zsa Zsa Gabor
7: Errol Flynn
8. Robert Taylor

Photo 1, courtesy of Dr. John Provan
Photos 2–8, courtesy of the SAS Museum, Oslo

CHAPTER 1
DONALD W. DOUGLAS: AIRCRAFT DESIGN VISIONARY

This rare photograph shows the barbershop in which Donald W. Douglas opened his first design office in 1920. Note the David-Douglas Company sign in the window on the right. *Courtesy of Douglas / Ron Handgraaf*

Published by Douglas, this overview shows the aircraft types produced by the company between 1921 and 1938. *Courtesy of Douglas / Ron Handgraaf*

Born in Brooklyn, New York, on April 6, 1892, Donald Wills Douglas started his business modestly in the backroom of a barber shop on Pico Boulevard in Los Angeles. The graduate of the Massachusetts Institute of Technology was one of the first designers with the aircraft manufacturer Glenn Martin when he decided to produce aircraft on his own in 1920. For his first project, Douglas partnered with wealthy Californian sportsman David Davis, who founded the Davis-Douglas Company to build the first aircraft capable of flying nonstop from the American West Coast to the East Coast. The resulting Cloudster took off from the US Army's March Field on February 24, 1921, on its maiden flight, thus establishing the long tradition of Douglas aircraft types. On June 27, 1921, with test pilot Eric Springer and David Davis on board, the aircraft took off from the West Coast and set course for New York. It got only as far as El Paso, Texas, however, where engine failure resulted in a forced landing. On May 3, 1923, Davis's dream of going down in the history books finally vanished into thin air after two US Army pilots made the first successful transcontinental flight. Davis immediately

DOUGLAS ROLL-CALL OF THE YEARS

Illustrating 15 out of 129 types developed by the Douglas Company 1921 to 1938

1921   The Cloudster—first plane built by the Douglas Co.

1924   One of four world cruisers built for the U. S. Army.

1926   Mail plane that pioneered routes for P. O. Department.

1927   Personnel transport built for the United States Army.

1929   Observation plane built for the United States Army.

1930   Observation plane for Army; many are still in service.

1931   Dolphin amphibian for Coast Guard and commercial use.

1934   DC-2, first production model of transports in world use.

1935   Experimental flying boat developed for the U. S. Navy.

1936   DST sleeper and DC-3, world standard transport introduced.

1936   Parasol type observation plane developed for the U. S. Army.

1937   Attack bomber built in quantities for the U. S. Army.

1937   Many of these bombers built for the United States Army.

1937   Torpedo dive bomber built for the United States Navy.

1938   DC-4, world's largest land plane sets future standards.

withdrew from the company, which went on to write aviation history as the Douglas Company, with Donald Wills Douglas as sole owner.

The company quickly outgrew the cramped conditions of its first temporary office and sought alternate homes for its drawing boards and growing staff in a planing mill, an empty airship hangar, and the stage of a movie theater until, in 1929, it found a long-term location for the design, production, and flight testing of its machines at Clover Field airfield in Santa Monica. By then, the company had been called the Douglas Aircraft Company for a year, with Donald W. Douglas still the sole boss. By 1939 the factory site covered 23 acres, and the buildings had a footprint of 1,315,974 square feet. But the expansion did not end there. In addition to Clover Field, other plants were soon added in El Segundo, Long Beach, Torrance, Tulsa, and Chicago. Donald W. Douglas remained the undisputed "boss" of the company throughout his life. He was respectfully described by Maj. Alexander Prokofieff De Seversky, an American aeronautical engineer of Russian descent, as the "cornerstone of American air power." Described as reserved, a perfectionist, and shying away from publicity, the company's founder insisted that his closest staff inform him daily about every detail of his business. While Douglas Sr. cultivated a management style based on reliability and mutual respect, his son Donald Douglas Jr., born on July 3, 1917, was exactly the opposite. The flamboyant and always provocative junior boss was introduced to the company in 1939, and his father began preparing him for his future role as head of the company. He took over control in 1957, when Douglas Sr., formerly both president and chairman of the board, transferred at least the role of president to Douglas Jr. The company management was shocked by the aggressive management style of the new boss and left the company in droves. In this difficult situation, it did not help that Douglas Sr. revised some of his son's decisions and that it was not clear which member of the Douglas family oversaw the company. Development costs of the first two Douglas jetliners, the DC-8 and DC-9, as well as production delays involving the twin jet, finally brought the Douglas Aircraft Company into a dramatic financial predicament in the mid-1960s, which improved only after its merger with McDonnell in April 1967. The now-seventy-four-year-old Donald Douglas Sr. remained associated with the resulting McDonnell Douglas company as honorary chairman of the board until his death on February 1, 1981. His son remained on the board until 1989 and died on October 3, 2004.

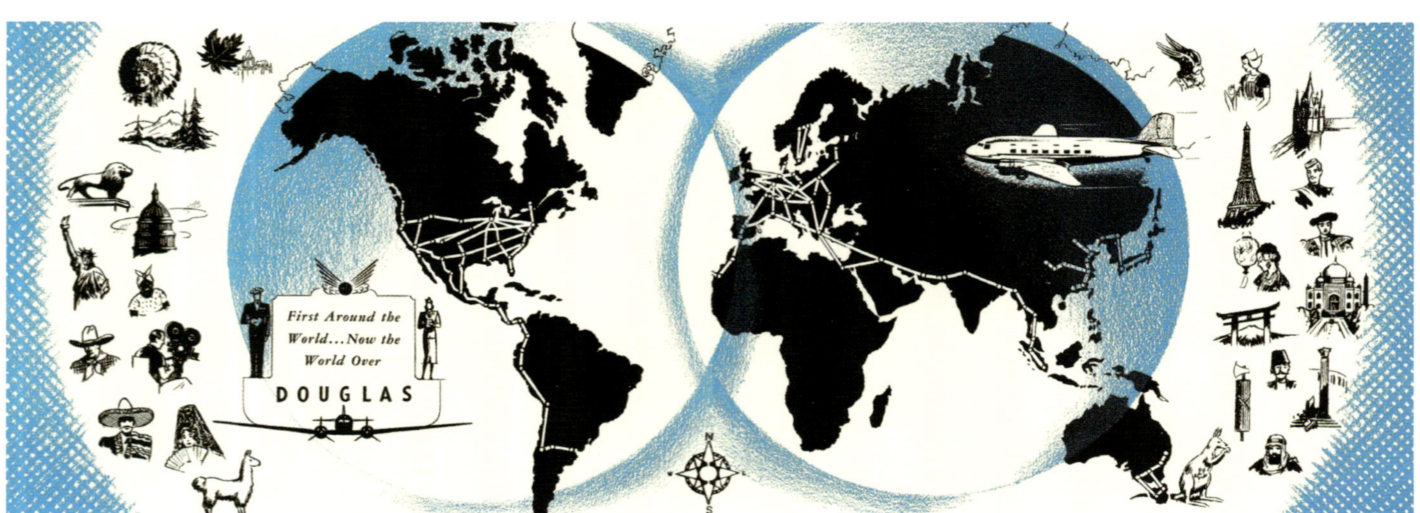

Douglas advertisement from 1938 for its DC-2 and DC-3, which were in service around the globe. *Courtesy of Douglas / Ron Handgraf*

CHAPTER 2
THE BEGINNINGS OF THE DOUGLAS COMMERCIALS

Captain's steering column of a Douglas DC-4. *Courtesy of SAS Museum, Oslo*

The impetus for the development of modern commercial aircraft by the Douglas Aircraft Company came from a competing product from Seattle, farther north, also on the US West Coast. The twin-engine Boeing 247 was one of the most advanced and fastest commercial aircraft of its day. In 1932, United Air Lines placed an order for sixty Boeing 247Ds with seating for ten passengers. The D version had various design improvements over the basic model, such as variable-pitch propellers, low-drag engine cowlings, and rear-facing cockpit windows. Another novelty: the first twin-engined commercial aircraft of low-wing design, the B 247, was able to maintain altitude on just one engine at full payload. Transcontinental & Western Air (TWA) showed interest in the type; however, Boeing could not guarantee delivery until after the fiftieth aircraft had been built, and TWA placed an alternative order with Douglas to build an aircraft type with an even-larger passenger cabin and better flight performance than that of the Boeing 247D. The result was the Douglas Commercial DC-1—forebear of the legendary DC-2 and DC-3 aircraft family.

The only Douglas DC-1 to be built, here in front of the art-deco-style terminal of the Glendale airport in California. *Courtesy of Douglas / Ron Handgraaf*

The prototype took off on its maiden flight on July 1, 1933, and the DC-1 received its type certificate just four months later. With its two 710 hp Wright Cyclone radial engines, it could carry twelve passengers—two more than the competing Boeing. The DC-1 was also faster and had a greater range than its archrival. The first customer, TWA, set a speed record between the East and West Coasts of the United States with this model on February 19, 1934, and it also ordered the larger DC-2, with 720 hp radial engines and a longer and wider fuselage. Production of the DC-2 totaled 156, and these aircraft flew with airlines in the United States, Asia, and Europe. In Europe, for example, the type flew in the colors of the Polish airline LOT, Iberia of Spain, Lufthansa, and, above all, the Dutch airliner KLM, which used its Douglas airliners for scheduled services between the Netherlands and the Dutch colony in what is now Indonesia. The next evolutionary step of the DC family came at the request of American Airlines president C. R. Smith. He planned to use an aircraft with fourteen double-decker beds on nightly transcontinental routes across the United States. The fuselage of the DC-2 was widened again, the cabin ceiling raised, the wingspan increased, and a new tail designed. The DC-3, initially called the Douglas Sleeper Transport (DST), was born. On December 17, 1935, the prototype of this model took off on its maiden flight. With 455 civilian aircraft sold and almost 20,000 military variants built, it is one of the most produced aircraft anywhere in the world.

After the completion of flight testing, Douglas delivered the first DST to American Airlines on June 7, 1936. The DC-3, designed to carry twenty-one passengers on daytime flights, followed two months later. United Air Lines, a Boeing subsidiary until 1934, took advantage of its new independence and became the second DC-3 customer in November 1936. TWA, Braniff, Pan American Airways, and KLM followed with further orders. By 1939, more than 90 percent of all domestic American air passengers were flying on DC-3s. The outbreak of World War II in September 1939—and, at the latest, the entry of the United States into the war in December 1941—led to a veritable boom in orders for the military variant, initially designated the C-47. From 1942, Douglas delivered 965 C-47s and 2,954 C-47As to the US Army Air Force (USAAF) from its new factory in Long Beach, California. A further 2,300 C-47As and 3,064 C-47Bs were produced in Oklahoma City. The C-47 differed from its civilian counterpart in that it had a large cargo door with structural reinforcements and a cabin adaptable for the carriage of troops or cargo with no sound insulation. There were countless versions of the DC-3 in military use, including eight type designations for those aircraft that had flown for airlines before their wartime service. In addition to powered versions on wheels, floats and skis, Douglas also developed a version for use as a cargo glider. It was planned that this Douglas XCG-17 would be towed by a C-47, but it never entered production.

Alongside the USAAF, which called its aircraft the Skytrain, and the US Navy's Skytrooper, the British Royal Air Force was one of the largest operators of the DC-3 series, which it christened the Dakota. RAF Dakotas earned a legendary reputation as "bombers" during the Berlin Airlift in 1948–49, when they helped supply the beleaguered city with all the essentials by air. In addition to the production lines in the United States, the DC-3 was also built under license in Japan and the USSR. In the Soviet Union

The Dutch airline KLM was an important customer for the DC-2. The aircraft named "Uiver" ("Stork") became legendary, winning the airliner category of the MacRobertson Air Race between London and Melbourne in 1934. *Courtesy of KLM*

This artistically appealing color postcard was issued in the 1940s by the Swedish airline AB Aerotransport (ABA). It shows passengers boarding their Douglas DC-3A-214. This Dakota bore the registration SE-BAB and was named "Höken" ("Hawk"). *Courtesy of ABA / author's collection*

By 1939, the Douglas Aircraft Company's modern production facilities in Santa Monica had already assumed imposing proportions. *Courtesy of Douglas / Ron Handgraf*

The DC-3 could be operated both as a passenger aircraft and a freighter. *Courtesy of Flughafen Stuttgart GmbH*

A Douglas DC-6 and a DC-3 of the British airline Air Atlantique in formation flight. Once based in Coventry, the airline continued to use its Dakotas even in the 1990s for nostalgia flights, as freighters, and as spray planes for fighting oil pollution of the seas. The DC-6s, on the other hand, were used as freighters and the stars of air shows. *Courtesy Air Atlantique / author's collection*

alone, a total of 6,157 Lisunov Li-2s were produced. During the Second World War, Russia also received more than 700 US-made DC-3s, equipped with Russian AS-62 engines and designated TS-62s.

FURTHER DEVELOPMENTS

After the end of the Second World War, airlines demanded new aircraft that were faster and larger than the hundreds of DC-3s and C-47s available from surplus military stocks. Spurred by the initially great interest of the airlines, Douglas then developed the Super DC-3. More-powerful engines, a longer fuselage for up to ten more passengers, a larger vertical stabilizer, and up to 50 percent more range turned the original DC-3 design into a new, elegant airliner. But in the end, Douglas was able to sell only three aircraft to Capital Airlines. Had the US Navy not decided to convert a hundred of its own standard DC-3s, designated R4D-5 and -6, into R4D-8 Super DC-3s, this program would have been a commercial flop.

The final DC-3 conversion, which is still offered today, is the Basler Turbo-67, developed by Basler Turbo Conversions. The company, based in Oshkosh, Wisconsin, replaces the DC-3's old Wright radial engines with modern Pratt & Whitney Canada PT6A-67R turboprops with Hartzell five-bladed propellers. A cockpit upgrade and further system improvements round out the overall package. Thus, made fit for the twenty-first century, the converted DC-3s not only can fly faster, higher, and farther than the standard version of 1935 but also carry even more payload.

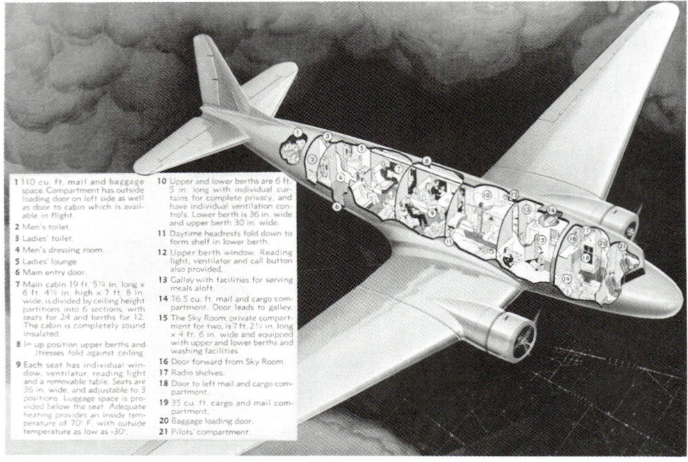

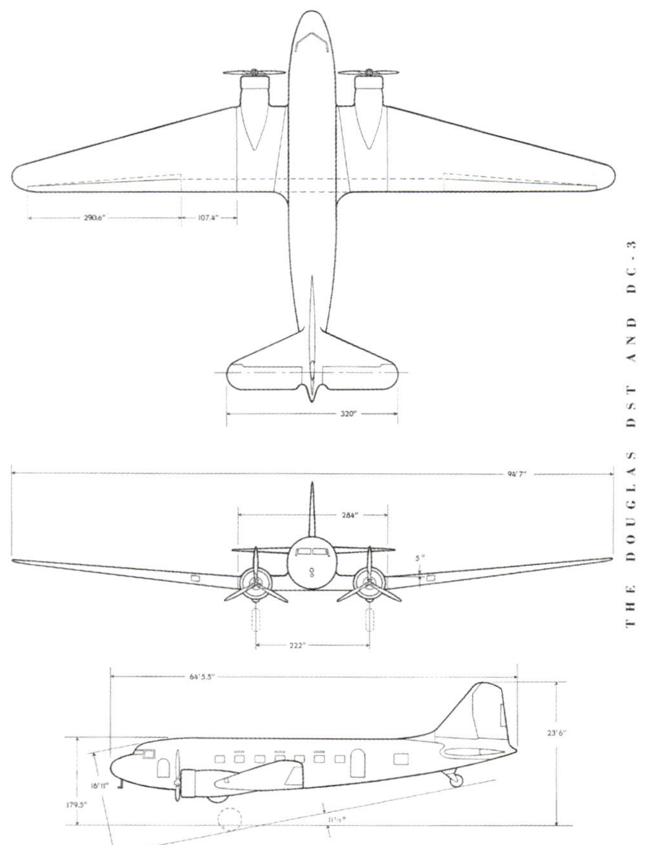

A Douglas Sleeper Transport (DST) as illustrated in a Douglas issued brochure dating back to the year 1938. *Courtesy of Douglas*

CHAPTER 3
THE DOUGLAS FOUR-ENGINED PROPLINERS IN DETAIL

DOUGLAS DC-4E EXPERIMENTAL

The Douglas Aircraft Company developed the DC-4 Experimental (DC-4E) by building on the design of the DC-3. In 1936, on the basis of a United Air Lines requirement, Douglas began construction of a four-engine luxury airliner for nonstop flights between its hub in Chicago and the metropolitan areas of North America's East and West Coasts. United was then joined by American Airlines, Eastern Air Lines, Pan American Airways (PAA), and Transcontinental & Western Air (TWA). Each of the five airlines contributed 100,000 US dollars to the development costs. Douglas knew that the advances from potential launch customers would never cover his own expenses, but the prospect of lucrative orders silenced all in-house doubters. Hoping for a major order from prospective customers, company owner Donald W. Douglas and his team began two years of development work, during which 1.5 million engineering hours went into the design of the aircraft—even after TWA and PAA had withdrawn from

This detailed cutaway drawing illustrates the cabin layout proposed by Douglas. *Courtesy of Douglas / Ron Handgraf*

the special-purpose group in favor of the cheaper Boeing 307 Stratoliner. After 866 wind tunnel tests using scale models, with a duration of 1,100 hours corresponding to 361 actual flying hours, the aerodynamic design of the DC-4E was finalized. The first Douglas four-engined propeller-driven airliner was strikingly similar to recommendations made by the engineers of the National Advisory Committee for Aeronautics (NACA), founded in 1915, for the design of a large commercial aircraft. This US governmental research institution was concerned with basic research for aviation and was a direct predecessor of the National Aeronautics and Space Administration (NASA), into which it was merged in 1958. For example, NACA optimized wing profiles in its own wind tunnel, resulting in the so-called NACA profiles, and developed the NACA cowling as an aerodynamic fairing for radial engines. In addition, in the early years its research supported technological innovations such as retractable landing gear, which the DC-4E also had. Its first location was the Langley Memorial Aeronautical Laboratory, named after rocket pioneer Samuel Langley, now NASA's Langley Research Center in the state of Virginia.

Like the Lockheed Constellation, the DC-4E had three vertical stabilizers, which were significantly lower than a single vertical tail, enabling the aircraft to use existing hangars. The DC-4E was not only the largest landplane built in the US at that time, but also the first with a tricycle undercarriage without the then-standard tailwheel. Called "Tri-Safety" by Douglas, the now-standard tricycle

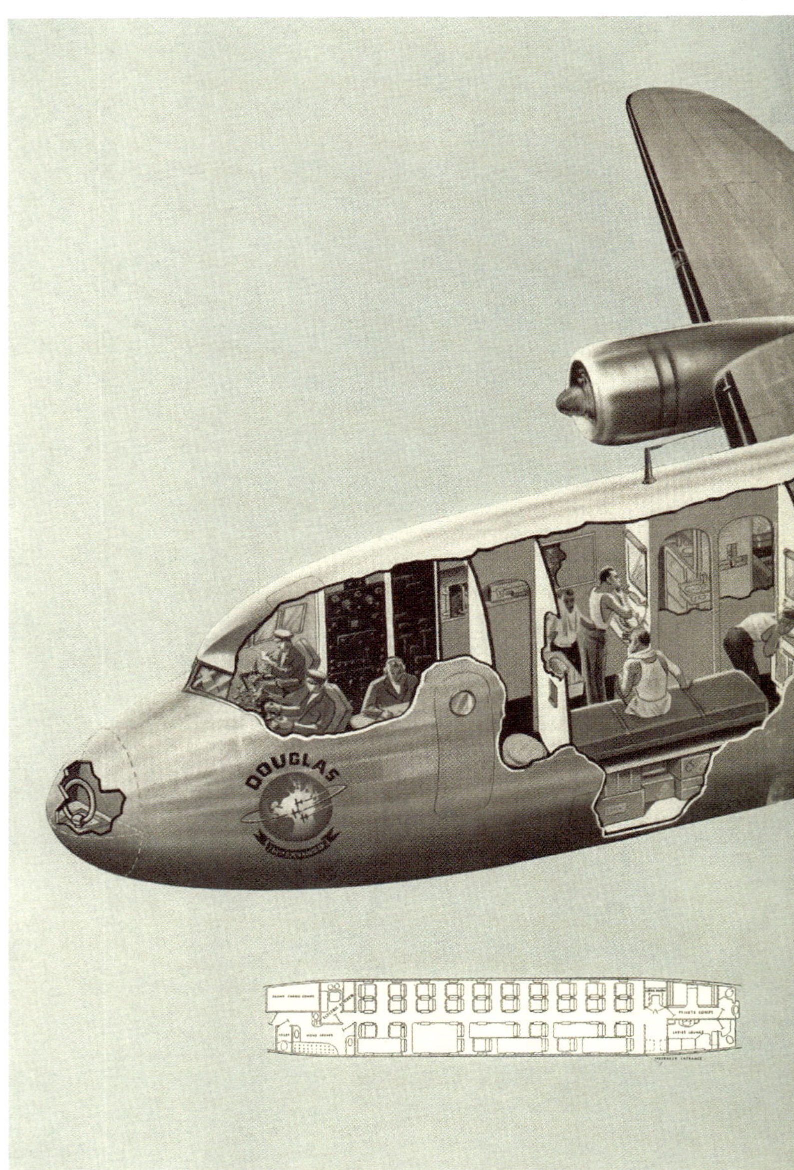

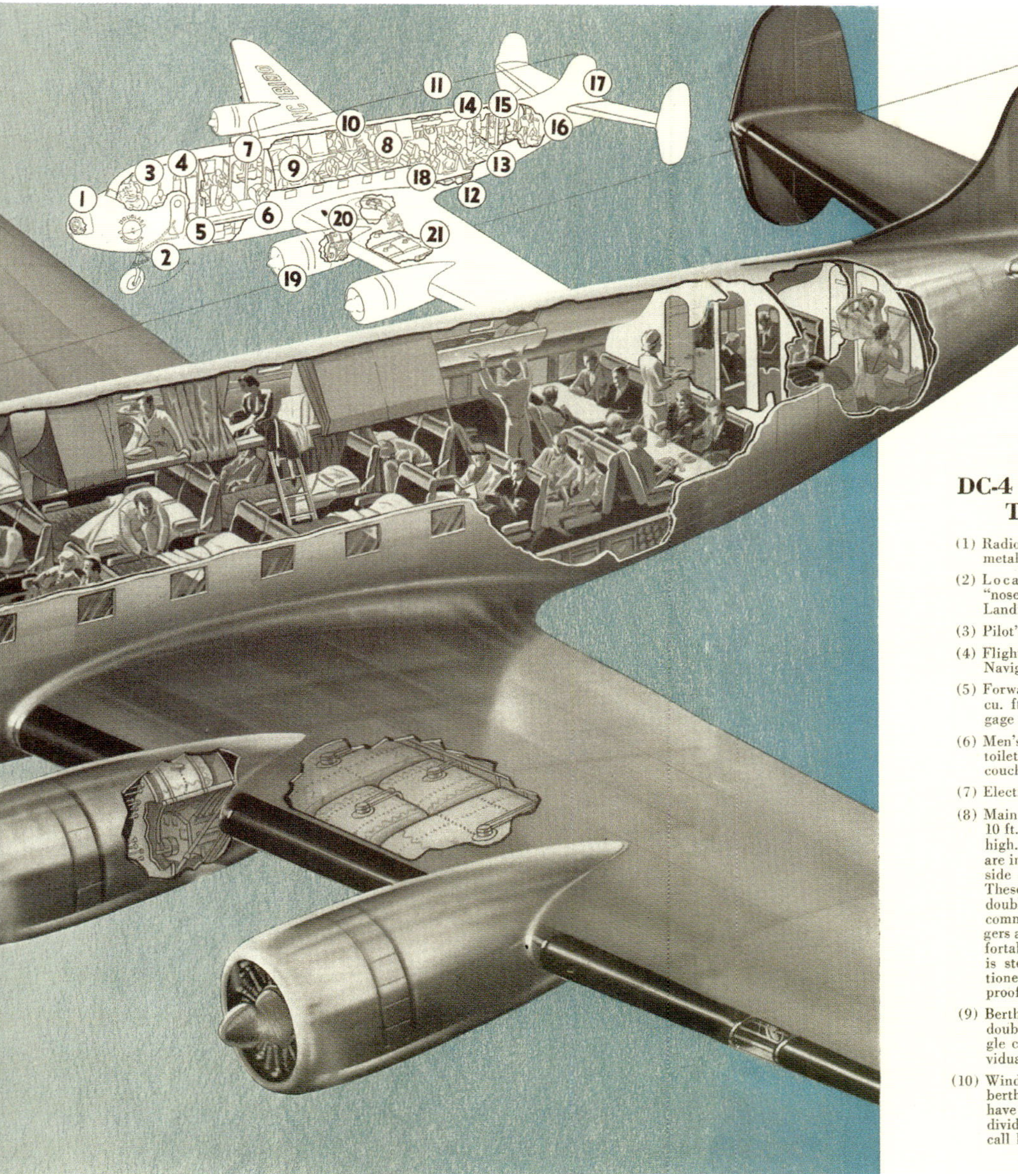

DC-4 CUT-AWAY DIAGRAM AND KEY TO GENERAL ARRANGEMENT

(1) Radio Loop Antenna in non-metalic nose section.

(2) Location of retractable "nose" wheel of Tri-Safety Landing Gear.

(3) Pilot's Compartment.

(4) Flight Engineer, Radio and Navigation quarters.

(5) Forward Cargo Hold. 326 cu. ft. space for mail, baggage and express.

(6) Men's Dressing Room with toilet, three wash basins and couch.

(7) Electric Kitchen.

(8) Main Cabin 41 ft. long by 10 ft. 9 in. wide by 7 ft. 6 in. high. Forty lounge chairs are installed in pairs on each side of the center aisle. These make up into single or double beds. Sleeping accommodations for 32 passengers are provided; 12 in comfortable upper berths. Cabin is steam heated, air conditioned and completely sound proofed.

(9) Berths can be made up for double occupancy or as single compartments with individual chair.

(10) Window in the sky. All berths, including uppers, have individual windows, individual reading lights and call buttons.

(11) Antenna.

(12) One of two rear Cargo Holds with total capacity of 210 cu. ft.

(13) Seat and table arrangement permits home comforts.

(14) Check Room for clothing and hand luggage.

(15) "Bridal Suite." De luxe section with private facilities.

(16) Ladies' Lounge. Everything for milady's boudoir in spacious, elegant seclusion.

(17) Douglas Triple "S" Tail. Stability, Strength and Safety assured by this feature.

(18) In flight these huge wheels are hydraulically retracted.

(19) Four main power plants with full feathering propellers give the plane 5,600 h.p. for take-off.

(20) Auxiliary Engines. Two of these generate power for lighting, cooking and hydraulic control.

(21) Fuel tank section. Each engine has individual tank as well as interchangeable supply from total of 2,050 gallons of fuel.

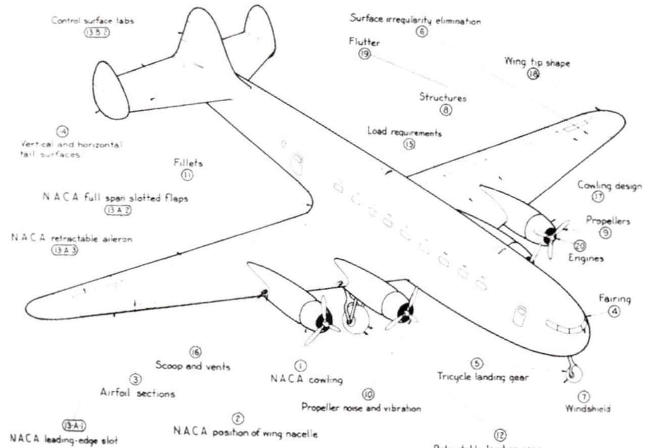

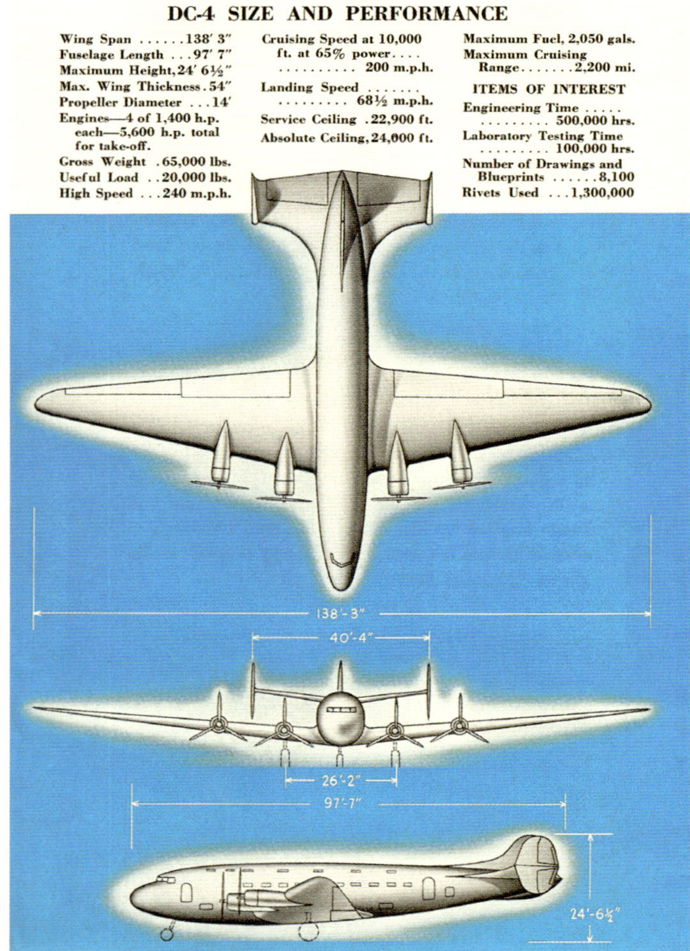

DC-4 SIZE AND PERFORMANCE

Wing Span . . . . . .138' 3"
Fuselage Length . . .97' 7"
Maximum Height, 24' 6½"
Max. Wing Thickness . 54"
Propeller Diameter . . .14'
Engines—4 of 1,400 h.p. each—5,600 h.p. total for take-off.
Gross Weight . 65,000 lbs.
Useful Load . . 20,000 lbs.
High Speed . . .240 m.p.h.

Cruising Speed at 10,000 ft. at 65% power. . . . . 200 m.p.h.
Landing Speed . . . . 68½ m.p.h.
Service Ceiling . 22,900 ft.
Absolute Ceiling, 24,000 ft.

Maximum Fuel, 2,050 gals.
Maximum Cruising Range . . . . . . .2,200 mi.

ITEMS OF INTEREST

Engineering Time . . . . 500,000 hrs.
Laboratory Testing Time . . . . 100,000 hrs.
Number of Drawings and Blueprints 8,100
Rivets Used . . .1,300,000

The DC-4E could not deny its design relationship to the DC-3 and the subsequent DC-4A. *Courtesy of Douglas / Ron Handgraf*

The proposal by NACA, the forerunner of today's NASA, for a modern airliner in the mid-1930s was amazingly similar to the DC-4E built by Douglas. *Courtesy of NASA*

This three-view drawing shows details of the DC-4E. With the Second World War looming, its dimensions were too large for the airlines. *Courtesy of Douglas / Ron Handgraf*

Like the Lockheed L-1649A Starliner, the fuselage of the DC-4E was attached to the completed one-piece wing. *Courtesy of Douglas / Ron Handgraf*

Uploads of 180,000 lbs. applied to outer and inner wing sections by pulleys operating over these steel superstructures and hydraulic jacks pushing up under wings. Each wing takes 90,000 lbs.

Hydraulic system inside plane tested by this control.

Downloads of 50,000 lbs. applied to engine nacelles on each side of plane reproducing weight and pull of engines. Total downloads 180,000 lbs.

In this "torture chamber," the DC-4E was put through its paces, and the stresses of takeoffs, cruising flight, and landings were simulated by using hydraulic rams. *Courtesy of Douglas / Ron Handgraf*

undercarriage enabled passengers to enter and exit a horizontally oriented cabin, a first in commercial aviation. This also simplified the loading of freight and mail, which then as now made an important contribution to the profitability of a flight. Douglas also extolled the improved flight characteristics during landing and takeoff compared to an aircraft with a tailwheel undercarriage. With a wingspan of 138 feet, 3 inches, and a fuselage length of 97 feet, 7 inches, not only was the DC-4E an imposing sight, but the production facilities used to build the all-metal aircraft were also record-setting. They included what was then the largest hydraulic press in the world, capable of forming metal with a pressure of 5,000 tons. Three stories tall, the press weighed 840,000 pounds. Another press used in construction of the DC-4E had a pressure of 2,000 tons.

Designed for a maximum range of 2,200 miles, which made it capable of nonstop flights between Chicago and San Francisco, the airliner was intended to augment the DC-3 and DC-5 and was equipped with every conceivable luxury. Among the highlights were a pressurized cabin and automatic steam heating, which ensured a constant cabin temperature of 70 degrees Fahrenheit. Two auxiliary power units housed in the wings also maintained pressure in the hydraulic lines and supplied the onboard power network with a voltage of 115 volts. This network supplied power not only to the instruments in the cockpit, but also to the cabin lighting, the cooker in the all-electric galley, and hair curlers in the "ladies lounge" and the electric razors in the "men's dressing room," as it says in a contemporaneous sales brochure for the DC-4E. The cabin was designed for a maximum of forty passengers on day flights and thirty-two passengers on night flights. On the latter, the flying luxury hotel was to be equipped with beds (so-called berths), which offered the highest level of comfort. Even a separate wedding suite for newlyweds was planned in the rear of the aircraft. The DC-4E was powered by four Pratt & Whitney engines with a combined takeoff power of 5,600 hp.

After Douglas had spent 1,634,612 US dollars in development costs, the prototype was ready to fly, and on June 7, 1938, it took to the air for the first time. Douglas had obviously scored a success with his experimental version because test pilot Carl Cover is said to have exclaimed enthusiastically after the landing: "She flies herself. I just went along for the ride." But by the time the only DC-4E to be built finally received its United Air Lines Super Mainliner livery in May 1939, the dark clouds of the Second World War were already gathering. The airlines consequently held back on orders, and even before the United States officially entered the war on December 8, 1941, Douglas developed the DC-4A, the familiar and, compared to the DC-4E, significantly smaller production version of its new model. The only completed DC-4E was sold to the Japanese airline Nippon Koku K.K. and served the Japanese aviation industry as inspiration for the Nakajima G5N Shinzan long-range bomber. After only six prototypes were built, the project was canceled, while the exported DC-4E crashed into Tokyo Bay shortly after its transfer from the United States to Japan and sank in its waters.

DOUGLAS DC-4A SKYMASTER

After the DC-4E, which though an excellent design was too large for its time, Douglas turned to the more compact and less complex DC-4A Skymaster as its first four-engined model to be produced in quantity. It was not as elegant a design, had a lower maximum speed, and, in contrast to the DC-4E and its direct competitor—the legendary Lockheed Constellation—did not have a pressurized cabin. And yet, the DC-4A was an important design that was to make a decisive contribution to the Allies' success in the Second World War. On February 14, 1942, the first Douglas C-54 troop carrier, the second DC-4 project, took off on its successful maiden flight. The first twenty-four aircraft built were still from prewar airline orders and were delivered to the US Army Air Force (USAAF) as C-54s. Only the following 252 aircraft were "real" military transports and received the designation C-54A. Of these, fifty-seven with the designation R5D-1 were passed on by the USAAF to the US Navy's Naval Air Transport Service (NATS). The

DC-4 ZS-AUB Outeniqua of South African Airways overflying Johannesburg in 1946. *Courtesy of SAR Publicity and Travel Department / Transnet*

By painting rectangular frames around the circular cabin windows of its DC-4s, Continentale Deutsche Reederei attempted to create the impression that the aircraft were more modern DC-6s with pressurized cabins. *Author's collection*

A DC-4 of the British airline Invicta visiting Copenhagen-Kastrup airport. *Courtesy of Tom Weihe*

C-54A was followed by 230 C-54Bs, equipped with integral fuel tanks in the wings and the ability to operate in the air ambulance role. Like the C-54A, the B version was produced in Santa Monica as well as in Chicago. NATS also received thirty aircraft from this order, which were used as R5D-2s during the Second World War. The USAAF gave one C-54B to the British Royal Air Force for use by British prime minister Winston Churchill as a personal transport. The fascinating history of the C-54C/VC-54C "Sacred Cow" as US president Harry Truman's first Air Force One is presented in a separate chapter. Further C-54 variants, such as the D, E, F, and G, followed as new factory models, while designations up to the C-54M were used for subsequently modified aircraft. The latter was used mainly on the Berlin Airlift in 1948–49. A separate chapter is also dedicated to these legendary "bombers."

THE YEARS AFTER THE SECOND WORLD WAR

Few postwar airlines did without the services of the Douglas DC-4 Skymaster. During this "Golden Age of Aviation," the propeller-driven airliners flew in the colors of the "Who's Who" of the aviation industry: from American Airlines, Canadian Pacific, Delta Air Lines, Pacific Western, Pan American Airways, Trans World Airlines, and United Air Lines in North America and Aerolineas Argentinas and Avianca in South America, to Air France, KLM, Sabena, SAS, Swissair, and Lufthansa in Europe—to name just a few of the best-known names. Civil Douglas DC-4s and those converted from military transports into commercial aircraft flew with airlines on the African continent, such as Aden Airways, Air Algerie, South African Airways, and Trek Air, as well as with Cathay Pacific in Hong Kong and Ansett, among others, and Qantas on the fifth continent. To list all the civilian operators would be far beyond the scope of this book. The same is true of its competitors, which include just about every long-range type of civil aircraft built in the 1930s and 1940s. After the end of the Second World War, Douglas had difficulty getting airlines to buy brand-new DC-4s. Too many used aircraft, which

Deutsche Aeroexpress marketed Continentale Deutsche Luftreederei's fleet of DC-4s and advertised a full charter with this ad. *Author's collection*

Greenlandair operated this DC-4 with the registration OY-DKG between 1967 and 1973. The aircraft was originally built for the US Army Air Force as a C-54E-DO. *Courtesy of Tom Weihe*

Stuttgart-Echterdingen airport was a regular destination for the Douglas DC-4s of Air France in the 1950s, linking Paris with the capital of the federal state of Baden-Württemberg and the home of such famous companies as Mercedes-Benz, Porsche, and Bosch. *Courtesy of Flughafen Stuttgart GmbH*

Servicing the engines of a Douglas DC-4 of South African Airways in 1947. *Courtesy of SAR Publicity and Travel Department / Transnet*

were now being offered in large numbers by the USAAF and US Navy for little money, flooded the market. Nevertheless, Douglas managed to sell seventy-nine examples of the DC-4 in the postwar years before production of civil aircraft switched to the DC-6.

In the immediate postwar years, around the globe the Skymaster carried more passengers than any other aircraft type of the time. A representative airline was Pan American Airways (PAA), founded by the charismatic Juan Terry Trippe in 1928. In the years 1945–46 it operated no fewer than ninety-two former C-54s obtained from American military stocks. The Douglas DC-4 was the first aircraft that, from April 1954 onward, Pan American flew on its Internal German Service (IGS) between Tempelhof Airport, located in the American sector of West Berlin, and the metropolises of the Federal Republic of Germany, founded in 1949. While Tempelhof was the operational IGS hub, PAA maintained its technical base at Frankfurt/Main. The reliable Douglas propeller-driven airliners served the Berlin routes for two years before being replaced by larger Douglas DC-6Bs. It was not until 1966 that the jet age finally arrived on Pan Am's Berlin routes, with the advent of the Boeing 727.

In West Germany, meanwhile, C-54s converted to civilian DC-4s played a major role in the development of tourist air transport—albeit sometimes with fraudulent undertones. Five charter airlines—Aerotour, Continentale Deutsche Luftreederei, LTU, Luftreederei Karl Herfurtner KHD, and Trans-Avia—relied on the Skymaster. In retrospect, however, the Lufttransport Union (LTU) was the only reputable company among them, while all the other participants gave the charter aviation industry of the time a very bad reputation through opaque financial transactions, bankruptcies, and accidents. This crisis of confidence in the young German air tourism industry also hit LTU hard, the airline having acquired its first DC-4 in March 1958 and its second in August 1959. Under its two new managing directors, Ahrens and Krauss, however, LTU succeeded in changing its strategic and financial course from 1960 onward, which not only saved the company but also allowed it to rise to become one of the most renowned European airlines.

The so-called "Skycoach" tourist-class cabin of a South African Airways DC-4 in 1960. *Courtesy of SAR Publicity and Travel Department / Transnet*

Lufthansa leased two DC-4/C-54s from the American airline Transocean for cargo flights between Germany and the United States. *Courtesy of Lufthansa*

Aircraft lined up on the ramp at Zurich, with a DC-4 of Trans World Airlines (TWA) in the foreground; behind it, an aircraft of the same type of the Dutch airline KLM, and a DC-3 of an unidentified airline. *Courtesy of ETH Zurich*

TWA
Trans World Airline
DEFENSE DE FUMER
SMOKING NOT ALLOWED
RAUCHEN VERBOTEN

Finally, Deutsche Lufthansa also temporarily relied on Douglas DC-4/C-54s to build up its transatlantic cargo business. Two aircraft, leased from the American company Transocean Air Lines, were put into service starting in December 1957 with US registrations and a livery similar to the rest of the Lufthansa fleet. The business was a profitable one, however, since about 30 percent of the world's airfreight volume was flown over the North Atlantic at that time. These two DC-4s were followed two years later by a Lockheed L-1049H of the Flying Tiger Line, until Lufthansa began operating its own cargo aircraft on long-haul routes for the first time in 1960 with the two L-1649As registered D-ALAN and D-ALUB, which had been converted from passenger aircraft into freighters.

DOUGLAS DC-6 CLOUDMASTER

With the DC-6 Cloudmaster, the Douglas Aircraft Co. once again succeeded in building on the success of its legendary products, the DC-3 and DC-4. Douglas urgently needed sales successes after secondhand Skymasters from army stocks flew around the globe, but only a few new aircraft were sold by Douglas after the end of the world war. A commercial breakthrough with a successful new model was therefore urgently needed, which Douglas undoubtedly achieved with the DC-6, of which 704 civilian and military versions were produced.

The DC-6 resembled its predecessor—the DC-4—in numerous details. A heavily modified DC-4 (C-54) powered by Pratt & Whitney R-2800-22W engines, with the US Air Force (USAF) designation YC-112, served as the prototype for the civilian DC-6 as well as its military sisters, the C-118 of the USAF and R6D-1 of the US Navy. This YC-112 entered the flight test program on February 15, 1946, making this the official first flight date of the DC-6 type. The DC-6 was very popular with airlines from the beginning, especially because of its pressurized cabin, which enabled the Cloudmaster to operate at higher cruising altitudes than its predecessor. On March 28, 1947, American Airlines and

Built in 1958, this DC-6A of the British airline Eagle Airways, with the registration G-APOM, was written off in a crash following a touch-and-go landing for crew training at Shannon airport on March 26, 1961. The crew of six was able to escape the burning aircraft unhurt. *Author's collection*

The DC-6 D-ABAH, which once flew in the colors of the German holiday airline Südwestflug, was still preserved in Germany in 2021 and could be used for weddings and family celebrations. However, there was no longer any thought of flight operations. *Author's collection*

The DC-6A with the registration G-APNP was operated by the British airline Air Ferry for three years between 1965 and 1968. This photo was taken at Copenhagen-Kastrup airport on July 30, 1966. *Courtesy of Tom Weihe*

شركة الاخوان للخدمات العربه
BROTHERS AIR SERVICES
7O-ABK

BALAIR
BALAIR
HB-IBZ
IBZ

On August 31, 1969, Tom Weihe managed to get this rare shot of a DC-6B of the Yemeni airline Brothers Air Services with the registration 7O-ABK. It was one of several DC-3s and DC-6s of the airline founded in 1966 in Aden, which was taken over by Alyemda in 1971. After further stations with airlines in the Caribbean, Canada, and Europe, the history of this aircraft came to an end after its last mission with Iscargo as a firefighting training object in Reykjavik. *Courtesy of Tom Weihe*

The DC-6Bs of the Swissair subsidiary Balair were very rarely used on flights to Scandinavia. The photographer was therefore fortunate to capture HB-IBZ, originally delivered to Swissair and transferred to Balair in 1961, at Copenhagen airport on September 17, 1969. *Courtesy of Tom Weihe*

The DC-6B of the Norwegian airline SAGA with the registration LN-MTV was one of two aircraft of this nowadays rather unknown, long-defunct airline. This photo shows it on a sunny July 26, 1971, at Copenhagen. *Courtesy of Tom Weihe*

The Norwegian airline Troll-Air acquired this DC-6B with the registration OY-EAO from Sterling Airways, whose livery is still recognizable. The short-lived Troll-Air was the successor to the equally luckless SAGA. *Courtesy of Tom Weihe*

Founded in 1946, Norway's Braathens S.A.F.E. prided itself on being the Scandinavian country's "flag carrier," since its archrival SAS was operated by three nations. However, this did not protect it from being taken over by SAS in 2002 after it fell into severe financial turmoil. This photo of the DC-6B LN-SUT was taken on July 18, 1968, and thus in happier days. *Courtesy of Tom Weihe*

A/S Fred. Olsens Flyselskap was the cargo branch of the Norwegian shipping company of the same name. Its DC-6As were used on charter flights around the globe. One of these was LN-FON, photographed in Copenhagen on May 7, 1967. *Courtesy of Tom Weihe*

LN-SUT
RAATHENS S·A·F·E
DC6

LN-FON
FRED. OLSEN FREIGHTER

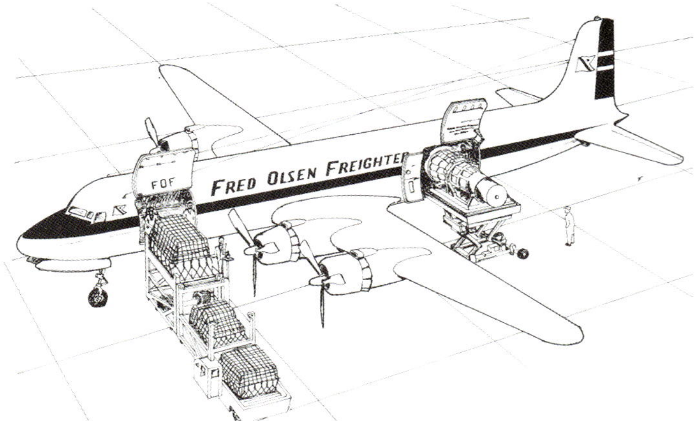

A/S FRED. OLSENS FLYSELSKAP

(FRED. OLSEN AIRTRANSPORT LTD.)

ALL-CARGO AIRCRAFT

P.O. Box 57, 1330 Oslo Airport, Norway — Telephone 53 09 00 — Telex Oslo 11645 Airnor

This schematic drawing shows the locations of the DC-6A's two cargo doors and typical loads. *Courtesy of Fred. Olsen / author's collection*

Fred. Olsen used brochures like this one to advertise charter services for its Douglas DC-6A cargo planes. *Courtesy of Fred Olsen / author's collection*

This historic photo of DC-6A LN-FOM shows cargo being loaded through the opened rear cargo doors. They allowed even very bulky cargo to be loaded. *Courtesy of Fred. Olsen / author's collection*

To protect the cabin sidewalls of the freighter, they were covered, and the cabin floors of this Fred. Olsen DC-6A were equipped with rollers for easier loading. *Courtesy of Fred. Olsen / author's collection*

United Air Lines took delivery of their first aircraft at Santa Monica, California. But the joy over the new additions to the fleet was short lived. A United Air Lines DC-6 on a flight from Los Angeles to Chicago crashed in flames in Bryce Canyon in the state of Utah, while a second American Airlines DC-6 burst into flames over New Mexico on November 11, 1947. While the United accident ended in disaster, the crew of the American Airlines aircraft managed to make an emergency landing. All occupants were able to leave the aircraft unharmed, and the flames were extinguished in time. In contrast to the first accident, investigators now had the opportunity to examine the airframe in detail and determine the cause. To avoid further accidents, all Douglas DC-6s that had already been delivered were grounded as a precautionary measure as early as November 12, 1947. It soon became clear that, due to a design fault, fuel flowing from the wing tanks had flowed into the heating devices for the passenger cabin and ignited. Douglas made efforts to rectify the fault quickly, and on March 21, 1948, almost a year after the first deliveries, the DC-6s were back in the air. The accidents and the subsequent grounding did not harm the type's popularity or the reputation of the Douglas company. This is perhaps in part because flying was generally much less safe back then, and crashes were therefore more common compared to today.

Even while the DC-6 was grounded, Douglas began developing further versions of the type with the designations DC-6A and DC-6B. Both variants had the same lengthened fuselage and greater range compared to the basic version. However, unlike the DC-6B, the DC-6A was designed exclusively for cargo transport. After their first flights, which took place on September 29, 1949 (DC-6A), and February 10, 1951 (DC-6B), the first freighters were delivered to Slick Airways and the first passenger aircraft to United Air Lines. Not least due to their robust construction and reliable Pratt & Whitney R-2800 piston engines, a small number of DC-6s were still in service as freighters on the North American continent in 2021, seventy-two years after the prototype's first flight.

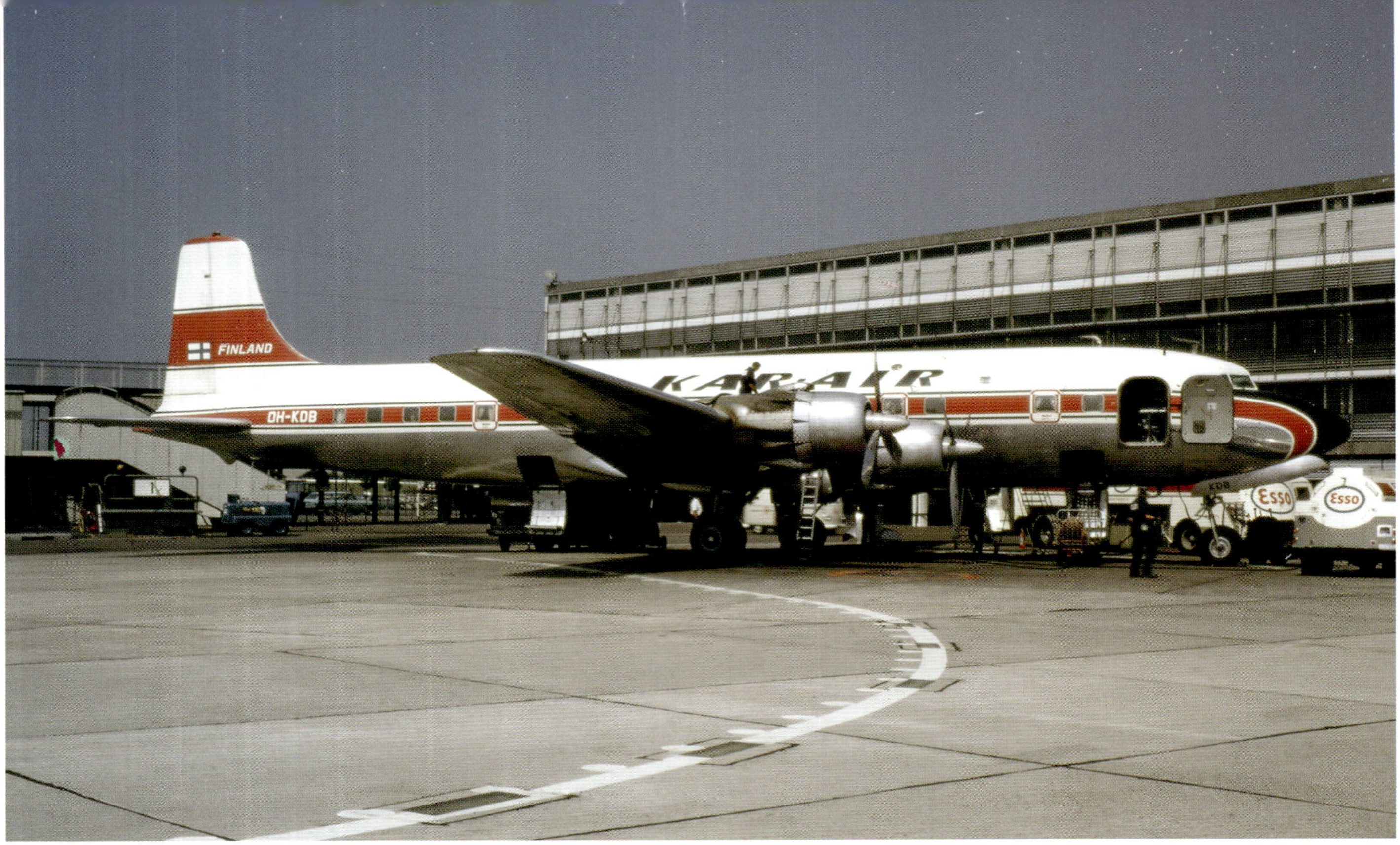

FINLAND
OH-KDB
KAR-AIR
ESSO

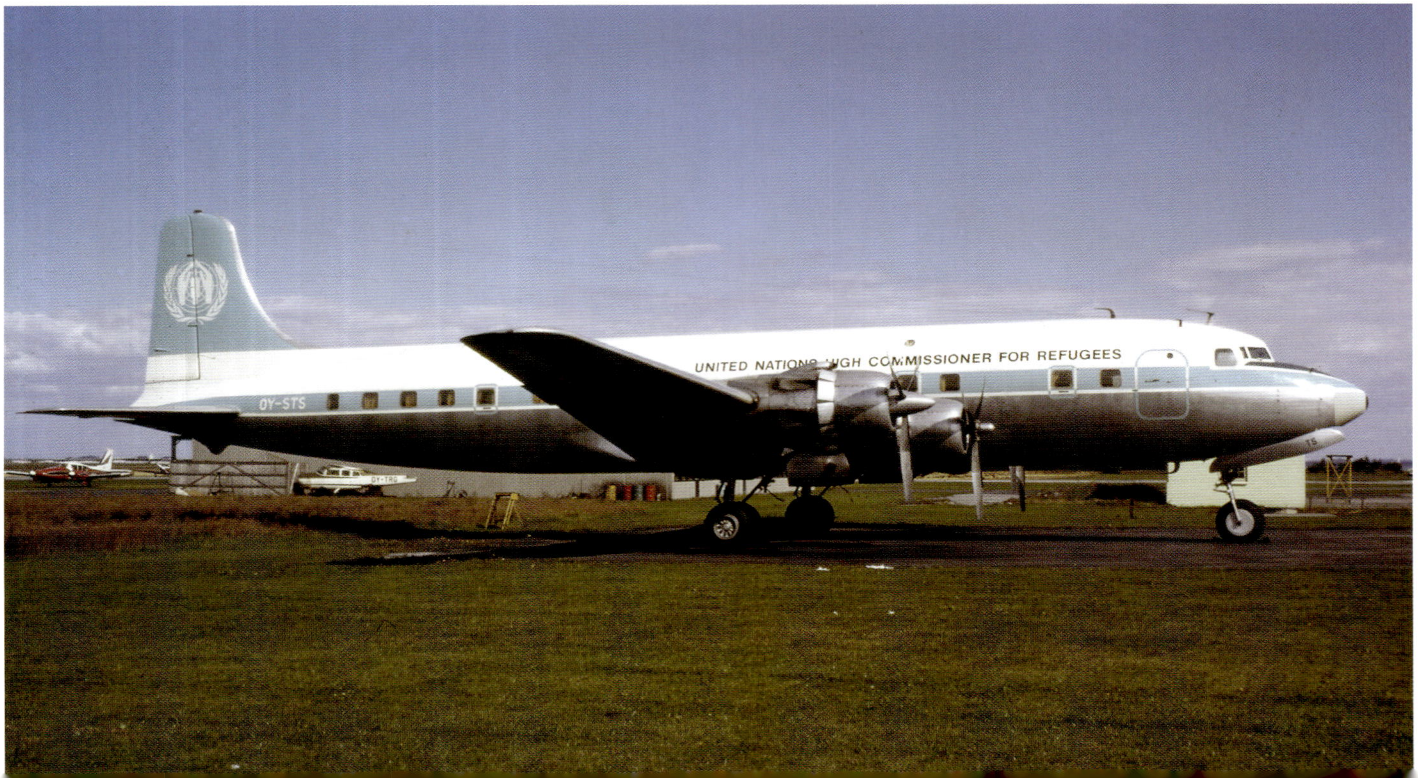

UNITED NATIONS HIGH COMMISSIONER FOR REFUGEES
OY-STS

The DC-6B with the registration OY-KDB, *shown here*, was one of three aircraft of this type operated by the Finnish airline Kar-Air, founded in 1947, until the 1970s. Its sister aircraft OH-KDA was unusual in having a folding tail for the loading of freight—analogous to the Canadair CL-44. *Courtesy of Tom Weihe*

Sterling Airways DC-6B, registration OY-STS, was used not only on charter flights, but also on behalf of the United Nations High Commissioner for Refugees. It was photographed in this special paint scheme at Copenhagen-Kastrup airport on August 27, 1972. *Courtesy of Tom Weihe*

DC-6B OY-BAS, the sister aircraft to the machine in the previous photo, photographed in regular Sterling Airways livery at Copenhagen on September 24, 1967. *Courtesy of Tom Weihe*

This cutaway drawing of a Douglas DC-7C Seven Seas provides a view of the Douglas long-range airliner's luxurious first-class cabin. *Courtesy of SAS / author's archive*

DOUGLAS DC-7C SEVEN SEAS:

THE GRAND FINALE!

The DC-7C was at the end of a long evolutionary chain of successful propeller-driven airliners produced by Douglas. The impetus for development of the DC-7 base model came from the president of American Airlines, C. R. Smith. He had earlier convinced Douglas to build the DC-3 in 1934 and thus laid the foundation for the success story of the aircraft manufacturer based in Santa Monica, California. Smith now demanded a further development of the DC-6B, which Douglas sent on its maiden flight on May 18, 1953, in the form of the DC-7. On November 4, 1953, an aircraft of this type was operated for the first time by American Airlines, making possible nonstop flights between the American East and West Coasts. Eastern Airlines initiated the DC-7B, which took off for the first time on April 21, 1955, and had a range roughly 560 miles greater than the standard DC-7. It was followed by the ultimate DC-7C Seven Seas long-range version, which took off on its maiden flight on December 20, 1955. Its primary distinguishing features from the DC-7B were extended wings to accommodate the extra fuel required for increased range, a slightly longer fuselage, and more-powerful engines with larger-diameter propellers.

Launch customer Pan American Airways (PAA) first used this type on April 18, 1956. This meant that the DC-7C was available about a year earlier than the Lockheed L-1649A Starliner, its direct competitor. The competition between Douglas and Lockheed as the two leading manufacturers of civil propeller-driven aircraft at the time continued, especially between the archrivals TWA, which was in the Lockheed camp, and PAA, which relied on Douglas. In the "Golden Age of Air Transport," every minute of time saved over the competition on the transcontinental routes between the American East and West Coasts was considered a great PR success. And so, TWA sent its Super Constellation and Starliner into the race against PAA's Cloudmaster, DC-7B, and DC-7C Seven Seas, not only within America but also on the North Atlantic. There, too, the major airlines fought an unofficial battle for the "blue ribbon" of the fastest connection. And occasionally, air traffic control also helped, letting the home carrier land first and sending the competition from overseas into a holding pattern.

The DC-7C was also operated by numerous airlines in Europe. Among them were the Italian airline Alitalia, the British BOAC, KLM of the Netherlands, Swissair, the French airline TAI, and SAS of Scandinavia. With it, the "Flying Vikings" established scheduled air traffic between Europe and Japan over the North Pole route, with a refueling stop in Alaska. This was a pioneering achievement in aviation history, which will be honored in detail in a subsequent chapter. The great circle route over the Arctic explored by SAS and first flown on November 15–16, 1954, using Douglas DC-6Bs, was the shortest connection between the US West Coast and Europe. PAA and TWA followed Scandinavian about three years later with their DC-7C Seven Seas and L-1649A Starliners.

The impressive performance figures for the last large Douglas propeller-driven airliner could not, however, hide the fact that the era of propeller-driven aircraft on long-haul routes was coming to an end with the dawn of the jet age. Less than two years after the DC-7C's maiden flight, BOAC opened commercial jet service over the North Atlantic with a de Havilland D.H. 106 Comet 4 on October 4, 1958. Only a few days later, on October 26 of that year, Pan American followed with the Boeing 707-120 "Clipper America." Passengers on board the new jets were not quite as comfortable as they had been in the days of propeller-driven aircraft, but they traveled almost twice as fast and much more quietly. The almost vibration-free Rolls-Royce Avon and Pratt & Whitney JT3 jet engines that powered the two jet pioneers were a blessing for the passengers compared to the piston engines of the classic propeller-driven airliners with their vibration and noise. In addition, the new jets flew much higher, far above the turbulence zones through which the propeller machines usually traveled.

This DC-7C of the Voyager 1000 Travel Club arrived at Copenhagen with charter passengers from the USA on July 28, 1969. DC-7s flown by Voyager 1000 and Nomads, two American travel clubs, made stopovers in the Danish capital on that day. *Courtesy of Tom Weihe*

This DC-7B was last flown for the Historical Flight Foundation in Eastern Air Lines livery with the registration N836D. On July 28, 1969, the day this photo was taken in Copenhagen, construction number 45345 was in service for the Nomads Travel Club from the United States. *Courtesy of Tom Weihe*

This DC-7F of the Dutch airline KLM, with the registration PH-DSE, came to Copenhagen on June 16, 1966, to pick up freight shipments. Unfortunately, there is no record of where the airfreight went. *Courtesy of Tom Weihe*

N836D

KLM

PH-DSE   KLM ROYAL DUTCH AIRLINES

The DC-7C with the registration EC-BCH of Trans-Europa Compania de Aviacion S.A., once based on the Spanish holiday island of Mallorca, was a popular photo subject of the still-young "aircraft spotter" scene in Europe in the 1960s. On June 10, 1966, it flew sun-hungry Danish tourists to the south. Trans-Europa existed from 1965 to 1982. *Courtesy of Tom Weihe*

TRANS EUROPA
EC-BCH

CHAPTER 4
VARIATIONS OF THE SKYMASTER

THE CANADAIR DC-4M

AND C-4 NORTH STAR

POWERED BY ROLLS-ROYCE

The Canadair North Star was not only one of the most important postwar projects of the Canadian aviation industry, but also a very special milestone in aircraft construction. In designing the North Star, Canadair adopted a method it would later use to create the CL-44, combining various aircraft components from another manufacturer with new engines and systems to turn a good design into an even better one. The construction of this hybrid version of a Douglas DC-4 and DC-6 with British Rolls-Royce Merlin in-line engines was the result of a request from Trans Canada Air Lines (TCA). It was looking for a suitable aircraft to replace the tried-and-tested Avro Lancaster bomber, which, however, having been designed as a bomber aircraft, was not entirely suitable for transporting passengers. In 1942, the Canadian Victory Aircraft Ltd. first began to convert an A. V. Roe (Avro) Lancaster bomber produced

Canadair initiated development of the Canadair DC-4M and C-4 North Star at the behest of the Canadian airline Trans Canada Airlines. Both types were based on the Douglas DC-4, but they were equipped with four British Rolls-Royce Merlin in-line engines, and the C-4 with a pressurized cabin. *Courtesy of Air Canada*

Among other things, the North Star was intended to replace the Avro Lancaster bombers that had been converted into commercial aircraft. The civil version of the Lancaster was called the Lancastrian. These aircraft were far too small and uneconomical to compete on the North Atlantic in the postwar years. *Courtesy of aviationancestry.co.uk*

under license into a transport aircraft. The Toronto-based company replaced the bomber's glazed nose with a longer streamlined metal fairing, removed the rotating turret located centrally on the fuselage, and installed an aerodynamically shaped tail cone in place of the rear gunner's power-operated turret. New cabin windows completed the package of modifications made on the aircraft, registered CF-CMS, which was based at Dorval, near Montreal in Canada, from March 1943 onward. The converted Lancaster was initially used by TCA during the Second World War as a mail and cargo aircraft on the Canadian Government Trans-Atlantic Air Service (CGTAS) between Canada and Great Britain. Its ability to transport even heavy loads over long distances was impressive. TCA quickly recognized the potential of such a "civil" Lancaster for passenger transport and by August 1944 had expanded its fleet to five aircraft of this type, which crossed the North Atlantic in both directions on three weekly flights. The Canadian passenger Lancasters were very comfortably equipped by the standards of the time. The soundproofed cabin could accommodate up to ten passengers, and cabin heating was of a high standard for its day. Each passenger had a personal reading lamp, a call button for the cabin crew, a fresh-air nozzle, and—since smoking on board was a matter of course at that time—an ashtray at his or her seat. Even hot meals could be prepared in a modern galley. A contemporaneous report highlights the colorful design of the cabin, which was surely also intended to conceal its cramped conditions. The ceiling and upper sidewalls were a shade of yellow, the lower sidewalls rust, the carpet mahogany, and the seats light green.

The Canadian concept of a "swords to ploughshares" conversion of the Lancaster bomber also convinced the British A. V. Roe, developer and original producer of this type, which went on to build machines for British Overseas Airways Corporation (BOAC). Twenty examples of the aircraft, now called the Avro 691 Lancastrian for the first time and built on the Lancaster final-assembly line, were used mainly for Asian and African destinations of the British long-haul airline, such as Singapore and Johannesburg.

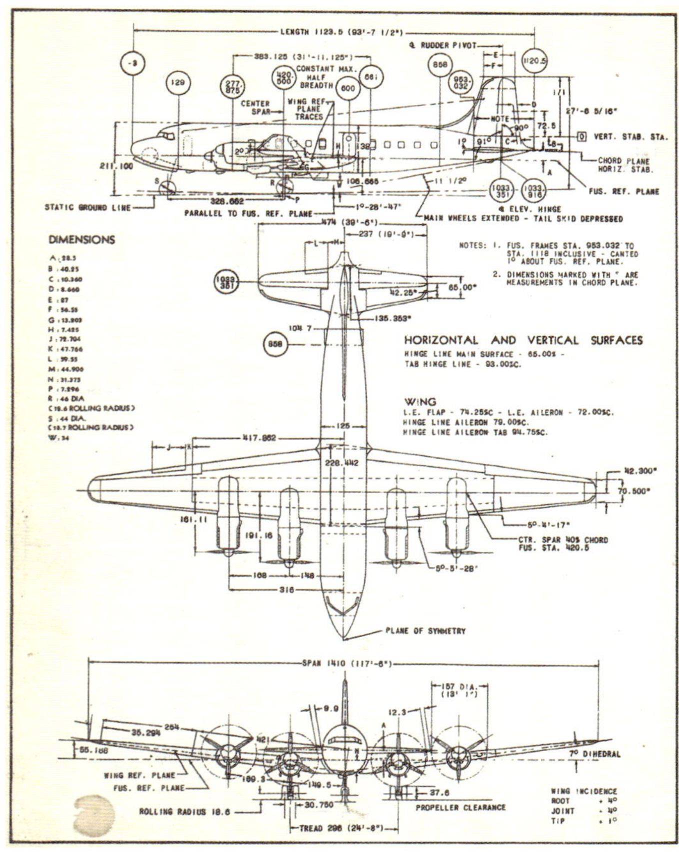

This drawing from the Canadair C-4 maintenance handbook illustrates the dimensions of the Canadian Douglas conversion. *Courtesy of Canadair / author's archive*

Pending delivery of the pressurized M2, Trans Canada Airlines borrowed six unpressurized DC-4M1 aircraft from the RCAF. Deliveries of the pressurized M2 began in October 1947, and the five surviving M1s were soon returned to the RCAF. The aircraft shown here, CF-TEK, was one of the M1s operated by TCA. *Courtesy of Air Canada*

The cockpit of the North Star was largely similar to that of the Douglas DC-4 and DC-6. *Courtesy of Air Canada*

A Trans Canada Air Lines (TCA) DC-4M2 overflying the airport at Bermuda. The aircraft seen here, CF-TFF, was delivered to TCA on December 19, 1947. *Courtesy of Air Canada*

Trans Canada Airlines DC-4M1 in flight over the Canadian capital of Ottawa. The unpressurized M1 can be recognized by its round cabin windows. In contrast, the pressurized DC-4M2 and the C-4 had the rectangular windows of the DC-6. *Courtesy of Air Canada*

The British overseas airline BOAC ordered twenty-two Canadair C-4s, which it named the Argonaut. The brochure shown here, distributed by BOAC, provided air travelers with information about the type. *Courtesy of BOAC / author's collection*

The days of the Canadair C-4 Argonaut and the Handley Page H.P. 81 Hermes (*shown here*) were supposed to numbered after the de Havilland Comet, the world's first jet airliner, entered service in May 1952. However, the grounding of the Comet in 1954 after a series of crashes caused by materials fatigue led to the immediate reactivation of both fleets. *Courtesy of the Society of British Aircraft Constructors / author's archive*

Argonaut

The Argonaut is outstanding among long-distance airliners both for comfort and excellence of performance. Flying in all parts of the world under all conditions, this famous airliner has built up a reputation second to none for regularity, smooth flying and dependability. Argonauts are in operation on the B.O.A.C. routes between Great Britain and West and East Africa.

Technical and Cabin information

LENGTH:	93 feet 8 inches
WING SPAN:	117 feet 6 inches
ALL-UP WEIGHT:	82,000 lb.
POWER UNITS:	4 Rolls-Royce Merlin, 12 cylinder inline liquid-cooled engines
CRUISING SPEED:	230/280 m.p.h. at a cruising altitude of between 10,000 and 20,000 feet
SEATING:	De Luxe sleeper-seats or reclinable armchairs, according to the Class of Service.
INFANTS' ACCOMMODATION:	Two Sky-cots are available and carry-cots may be obtained on request.
DRESSING ROOMS:	Cosmetics and toilet requisites are among the amenities provided in the dressing rooms and toilets.
AIR-CONDITIONING:	Automatic air-conditioning by remote control effects a complete change of air in the cabins every three minutes. In addition, each seat row has two ventilators under the individual control of passengers.
PRESSURIZATION:	Cabin pressure at 15,000 feet is usually maintained at the equivalent of 8,000 feet, although this can be reduced to 4,500 feet if required.
TEMPERATURE CONTROL:	A heater or refrigerating plant is used for heating or cooling the atmosphere as required.

British South American Airways Corporation (BSAA) was another customer for new aircraft from the factory. The first of eighteen Lancastrian 3s was delivered to BSAA in December 1945, and the type was used with great success on the airline's extensive route network between Great Britain and Latin America. The Lancastrian also played an important role in the Berlin Airlift in 1948 and 1949. After the Russians cut the overland links to the western zones of Berlin, over which supplies of vital materials such as food, coal, and petrol flowed, a considerable fleet of Lancastrians owned by BSAA, Skyways, and Flight Refuelling helped supply the Berlin population, mainly with liquid fuels, by air on behalf of the British Royal Air Force.

THE CHOICE FALLS ON DOUGLAS

In search of alternatives to the civil Lancaster, a TCA team visited the largest US aircraft manufacturers in 1943; however, it failed to find a design for a commercial aircraft that met its requirements and would be available in the anticipated postwar period. Of all the models offered, including civil versions of the Boeing B-29, Consolidated B-32, and Douglas C-74 Globemaster, the Douglas DC-4A and Lockheed L-049 Constellation came closest to meeting the Canadians' requirements. Detailed studies of the estimated operating costs showed that only an improved DC-4A would be economically viable on the TCA route network. In 1944, the Canadian government obtained permission from Douglas to build an aircraft in Canada by using components from the DC-4 and the DC-6, which until then had existed only on paper. The choice of engine was left to TCA, which planned to use its new airliner on Canadian domestic routes, routes to the US, and transatlantic flights. A TCA document dated July 13, 1944, lists the piston engines reviewed for suitability: Pratt & Whitney R-2000-9 and R-2800-C, Rolls-Royce Merlin and Griffin, Bristol Hercules, and Wright R-2600-22. In the end, after detailed analyses, all the candidates were eliminated except for the Pratt & Whitney R-2800-C radial engine and the Rolls-Royce Merlin in-line. Ultimately, a final comparison tipped

the scales in favor of the Rolls-Royce Merlin 620. The Merlin engine family was developed in the 1930s and was used to power numerous British aircraft types of the Second World War. These included the legendary Hurricane, Mosquito, Spitfire, and Lancaster. Built under license by Packard in the United States, the Merlin was also used to power the North American P-51 Mustang. The Rolls-Royce engine was also installed in British transport and commercial aircraft such as the Avro York and the Avro Tudor. In contrast to the air-cooled radial engines in widespread use at that time, the Merlin was a liquid-cooled, twelve-cylinder, four-stroke engine. Its two-cylinder blocks, each consisting of six cylinders, were arranged at an angle of 60 degrees in a V configuration.

Canadair Ltd. emerged toward the end of the Second World War from Canadian Vickers, which had ceased production when its major military contracts expired. The company initially stayed afloat by converting Douglas C-47 military transports into civilian DC-3s for customers in North America and Europe, until its management learned of TCA's plans for a new commercial aircraft. Originally, the Canadian government intended to award the construction of the DC-4/DC-6 hybrid to Boeing of Canada in Vancouver. But Canadair had already acquired the production facilities of the American DC-4 (C-54) plant in Parkridge, Illinois, from Douglas. Included in this package were about seventy C-54 fuselages, which served as the basis for the first TCA aircraft without pressurized cabins. And so, Canadair in Cartierville, near Montreal, was awarded the contract for the development and production of what would henceforth be called the DC-4M. Although it was initially "only" a conversion of existing aircraft, the development of the DC-4M1 posed great challenges not only for Canadair but also for Douglas and TCA. Douglas delivered 30,000 design drawings from California alone to Canada, to which Canadair added thousands of its own design drawings. The cabin design was entirely in the hands of TCA, whose team first built a cabin mockup in which various ideas were tested for their practicality. A Canadair team was also sent to Rolls-Royce in Great Britain to familiarize itself with the Merlin engine.

At the beginning of 1946 the first aircraft, with the registration CF-TEN-X, was slowly taking shape on the final-assembly line. This DC-4M1 without a pressurized cabin was intended for the Royal Canadian Air Force, but, like five other examples of this version, it initially entered service with TCA on transatlantic flights pending availability of the pressurized M2. On July 15, 1946, the champagne corks were popping in Cartierville after the successful maiden flight of the aircraft, which had been christened the North Star. Since Douglas feared that the Canadian product could compete with their own DC-6, Canadair was permitted to sell the DC-4M only in countries of the British Commonwealth of Nations. The buyers of this aircraft were also contractually prohibited from selling their aircraft to other airlines before the expiry of a period of two years or 5,000 flight hours. This unusual clause alone shows that Canadair had obviously hit the jackpot with the DC-4M.

In May 1947, the North Star was first presented to a delegation from the British Overseas Airways Corporation (BOAC), which was looking for a modern aircraft for BOAC's long-haul routes. The Handley Page H.P. 70 Halton and Avro 691 Lancastrian, bombers converted into passenger aircraft, and the Avro 685 York troop carrier, converted for airline operations, were only interim solutions for BOAC. The Tudor, newly developed by Avro in Great Britain, had a disappointing performance and was rejected by BOAC. So, in this case the British government discarded its maxim of "Buy British" and approved "Buy Commonwealth" in Canada as the second-best solution. On September 30, 1948, BOAC announced the purchase of twenty-two Canadair C-4s, which it was to operate as the Argonaut. Like the DC-4M2s of TCA and Canadian Pacific (CPA), BOAC's C-4s had the pressurized cabin of the Douglas DC-6. The BOAC Argonaut with the registration G-ALHK and the name "Atalanta" became famous. On January 31, 1952, Princess Elizabeth and the Duke of Edinburgh took off from London aboard this aircraft on a planned tour of the East African states. Elizabeth left England as a princess and, a few days later, after the death of her father, King George VI, returned to Great Britain on "Atalanta" as Queen

of England. BOAC was impressed with the reliable Argonaut and operated the Douglas-Canadair hybrid until 1960. Only the problem of the almost unbearable noise levels in the forward cabin area, caused by the exhaust system of the Rolls-Royce engines, could never be solved to the satisfaction of Canadair's airline customers. Knowing that piston engines generally caused much more noise and vibration in the passenger cabin than today's jets and turboprops, and that passengers were accustomed to leaving the aircraft with their hearing impaired after a long-haul flight, one can well imagine that the Merlin noise problem, perceived as particularly serious by BOAC, must indeed have been "deafening" in the truest sense of the word. Both TCA and BOAC adopted crossover exhaust systems—TCA's developed by Merlin "Mac" MacLeod and BOAC's based on Canadair research—to reduce noise. The exhaust gases from each cylinder were collected from both cylinder blocks and fed by a pipe system to the side of the engine facing away from the fuselage. The crossover exhaust system directed not only the exhaust gases away from the fuselage, but also some of the noise from the exhausts.

The gradual phasing out of the Canadair C-4 fleet had already begun following the introduction of the world's first jet airliner, the de Havilland D.H. 106 Comet 1, in 1952. On August 21, 1952, Comet jets replaced the much-slower Argonaut on the route between London and Colombo, followed by Singapore on October 14 of that year. Tokyo followed on April 3, 1953, and starting on October 1, 1953, Handley Page H.P. 81 Hermes replaced all Canadair C-4s on the Africa route network. BOAC was on its way to becoming an "all jet" airline, with the further-developed Comet versions 2 and 3 in its order books, when disaster in the form of two crashes caused by material fatigue in the spring of 1954 resulted in the grounding of all versions of the Comet. Deprived of the flagship of its long-haul fleet, BOAC fell back on its mothballed Argonaut and Hermes piston-engined airliners. What was initially intended as a short-term reactivation of the aircraft turned out, as so often in life, to be the best long-term solution! But even after the retirement of the last flying aircraft in April 1960,

North Star CF-TFN was a DC-4M2 with pressurized cabin. It joined the TCA fleet on March 5, 1948, and on July 1, 1961, was sold to the British airline Overseas Aviation. After subsequently serving with Keegan Aviation, it was scrapped at Luton Airport in the summer of 1964. *Courtesy of Air Canada*

The air intakes of the Rolls-Royce Merlin in-line engines can be seen particularly well in this photograph. *Courtesy of Air Canada*

The C-4 Argonaut with the registration G-ALHU is still wearing the basic BOAC livery in this photograph, but it was already flying for Overseas Aviation when it visited Hamburg airport. *Author's archive*

Overseas Aviation had outfitted the passenger cabin of the Canadair C-4 Argonaut G-ALHU with higher-density charter seating. *Authors archive*

it was to take another ten years before BOAC finally parted with its last Argonaut. During this period, G-ALHL "Arcturus" served the BOAC Apprentices Training Unit, helping train prospective mechanics. It was not until spring 1970 that "Arcturus" was replaced by a decommissioned de Havilland Comet 4 and passed on to the London Heathrow Airport Fire Brigade for training purposes. In contrast to G-ALHL, most of the BOAC aircraft found a new home with smaller British airlines such as Air Links, British Midland, Derby Airways, and Overseas Aviation, as well as the Danish charter airline Flying Enterprise, and for many years carried mainly sun-seeking charter tourists to destinations around the Mediterranean. Other aircraft went to Africa to Aden Airways, East African Airways, and the Royal Rhodesian Air Force. The last airworthy civil North Star, however, flew in North America and was taken out of service only in 1975 by a small cargo airline called Turks Air, based in the British overseas territory of Turks and Caicos Islands, southeast of the Bahamas, and subsequently scrapped. Only one North Star, an unpressurized C-54GM military version, has survived to this day. Its restoration by a group of volunteers from the Canadian Aviation Museum in Ottawa, which began in 2003, was well advanced in 2021 but not yet completed. This aircraft, with construction number 122 and the former Royal Canadian Air Force (RCAF) serial 17515, commemorates the second success story—in service with the Canadian Air Force. Taken on strength on March 8, 1948, this North Star remained in service with the RCAF until the type was decommissioned

at a stand-down ceremony in Trenton on December 8, 1965. Signed over to the Canadian National Aviation Museum just one year later, it spent thirty-nine years at Rockcliffe Airport, where it was parked outdoors and exposed to wind and weather. It was not until 1988 that the exhibit was moved to the vicinity of the current restoration hangar, where it has been kept inside since 2005. The goal of the Project North Star Association of Canada team is to restore the unique aircraft to "as-delivered flying condition"—but without aiming for airworthiness. All work is carried out to meet museum artifact conservation policies, using manufacturer's instructions and methods developed by the aviation and museum industries. This task is being accomplished under the direct supervision of the project manager, who is a licensed aircraft maintenance engineer. For example, the engines have been overhauled down to the last screw but do not have an airworthiness certificate. The North Star served as a reliable and versatile workhorse for the Royal Canadian Air Force. The museum's unique specimen was active in many vital roles, including northern resupply, research, training, relief operations, United Nations worldwide operations, support of Canada's NATO operations in Europe, and the famous and highly successful Operation Hawk airlift of supplies and personnel during the Korean War in 1950–53. It served with No. 426 Thunderbird Squadron RCAF until 1962, when the squadron stood down and most of its aircraft were retired from service. Just a few North Stars were retained in RCAF service until 1965, including 17515.

Trans-Canada Airlines North Stars were used for all types of services, including official visits by members of the government to other countries. *Courtesy of Air Canada*

VERSIONS OF THE NORTH STAR

C-54GM / DC-4M1

Transport aircraft operated by the Royal Canadian Air Force, nonpressurized

POWER PLANTS   four Merlin 622s with three-blade propellers

DC-4M2-3

Passenger version operated by Trans Canada Airlines, pressurized

POWER PLANTS   four Merlin 622s or 722s with four-blade propellers

DC-4M2-4

Passenger version operated by Trans Canada Airlines, pressurized

POWER PLANTS   four Merlin 624s or 724s with three-blade propellers

DC-4M2C

Freighter operated by Trans Canada Airlines

POWER PLANTS   four Merlin 724s with three-blade propellers

C-4 Argonaut

Passenger version for British Overseas Airways Corporation, pressurized. BOAC operated twenty-two Argonauts.

POWER PLANTS   four Merlin 624s or 724-C1s with three-blade propellers

C-4-1

Passenger version similar to the BOAC Argonaut, with modifications for operation by Canadian Pacific Airlines. Four aircraft were built.

POWER PLANTS   four Merlin 724s with three-blade propellers

C-4-1C

Trans Canada Airlines cargo version, conversions of two former Canadian Pacific Airlines C-4-1 passenger aircraft

POWER PLANTS   four Merlin 724s with three-blade propellers

C-5

Single example with the serial number 171. VIP aircraft delivered to 412 Squadron of the Royal Canadian Air Force on July 29, 1950. Equipped with just twenty-seven seats and a pressurized cabin, the aircraft remained in service with the RCAF until August 28, 1966. It was the only version of the North Star powered by much-quieter Pratt & Whitney radial engines instead of the noisy Merlin. Its fuselage was lengthened compared to the basic C-4 model, and it was fitted with the DC-6's strengthened undercarriage.

The ATL-98 with the registration G-ASHZ was the ninth Carvair built. One of the regular destinations of this flying English Channel ferry was the Dutch port city of Rotterdam, where the converted DC-4, bearing the name "Maasburg," was photographed on April 26, 1967, a bright, sunny day. *Courtesy of Tom Weihe*

This in-flight photo of the ATL-98 is remotely reminiscent of a Boeing 747. The fact that both cockpits are located on the "upper floor" has the identical reason, because only in this way could an undisturbed loading through the nose be guaranteed. *Author's archive*

AVIATION TRADERS ATL-98 CARVAIR

THE FLYING CAR FERRY

The Aviation Traders Ltd. -98 (ATL-98) Carvair is one of the most unusual aircraft of the "Golden Age of Aviation." It owes its creation to the British aviation pioneer Sir Freddy Laker. In the 1950s, he was not only a director of the airline British United, but also the owner of Aviation Traders Ltd., a company he founded in 1947 to trade in war-surplus aircraft and spares. He had already demonstrated his skills in special conversions in 1953, converting Avro Tudor aircraft into more-powerful Super Trader cargo aircraft. When British United was looking for a larger successor to the Bristol 170 for its combined passenger car service across the English Channel, Laker again brought his Aviation Traders into play. The twenty-one ATL-98s produced, whose name Carvair is derived from car-via-air, were based on nineteen Douglas C-54 military transports and two civilian DC-4 commercial aircraft. With its newly designed nose section, including the DC-4 cockpit moved up one floor, at first glance the Carvair looks like an early predecessor of the Boeing 747 Jumbo Jet. In fact, the motivation for this design was identical for both types, since both Aviation Traders and Boeing had the loading of large-volume cargo through the nose in mind. Other concepts, such as the Canadair CL-44 and the DC-6 freighter operated by Kar-Air of Finland, envisaged loading through a folding tail. The ATL-98 was consistently designed as a combined car-and-passenger transport, although some examples were used as pure freighters. While the passengers boarded via the rear passenger door in the forward-separated cabin area, the airline personnel loaded the Carvair with the cars and motorbikes through the open nose. In contrast to the jumbo freighter, whose nose folds upward and thus clears the way to the main deck, the Carvair's folding nose swings to the side.

Up to five medium-sized cars and a maximum of twenty-three passengers could be accommodated on board the ATL-98. The British United Subsidiary Channel Air

After a conversion time of 9.5 months, the Douglas C-54A-15-DC with the military serial 42-72246 flew for the first time as Carvair number "12" with the new registration G-AOFW on February 11, 1964. It is seen here in the livery of British Air Ferries. The photograph was taken at Jersey Airport on August 30, 1972.
Courtesy of Tom Weihe

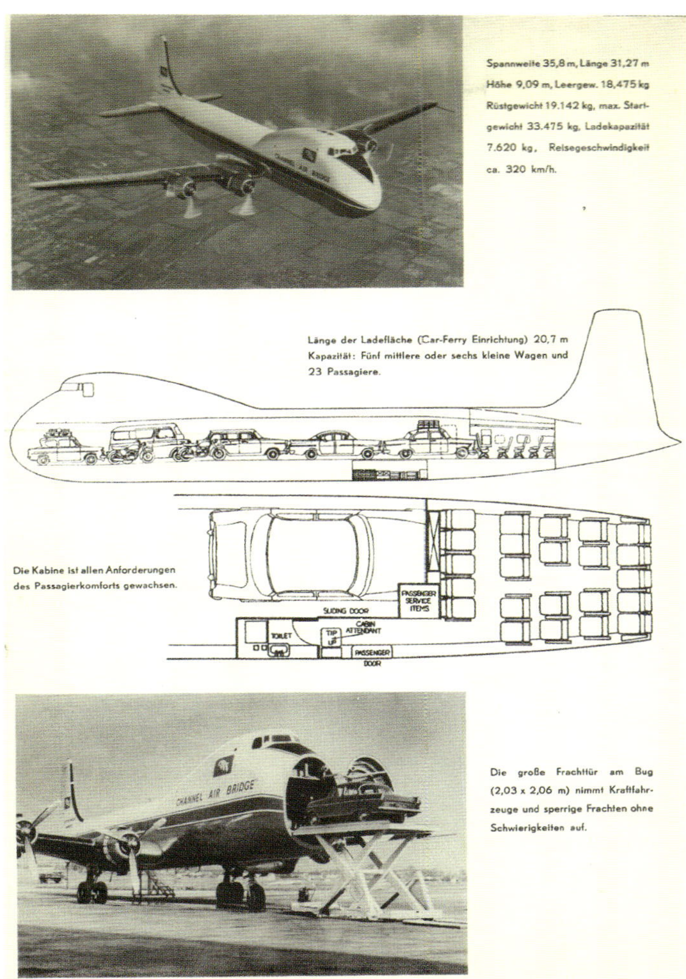

Published by Channel Air Bridge, this leaflet shows the cargo area and passenger cabin layout of the ATL-98. *Author's archive*

Bridge took delivery of the first ATL-98, christened "Golden Gate Bridge," on February 16, 1962. Renamed British United Air Ferries (BUAF) in January 1963, the airline was based at Southend, Southampton, and Lydd airports in southern England. In the summer of 1963, BUAF carried an average of 810 cars and 3,400 passengers per day across the English Channel to French, Dutch, and Belgian coastal towns. Other routes also took BUAF's Carvair fleet deep into the European hinterland, as far as Basel, Strasbourg, and Geneva. The twenty-one ATL-98s built flew with seventy-five airlines based around the globe. The last ones were used in the United States and South Africa until their retirement. In 2021, two complete ATL-98s still survived—as well as components of a number of aircraft.

The ATL-98 was operated by the Canadian airline Eastern Provincial Airways as a freighter. *Courtesy of David Johnston*

THE TWENTY-ONE ATL-98S THAT WERE BUILT AND THE DC-4 AIRCRAFT ON WHICH THEY WERE BASED

Carvair One	c/n 10528-1
Original aircraft	Douglas C-54B-1-DC
Delivered to the US Army Air Force:	January 22, 1945
USAAF serial	42-72423
Premodification operators	Braniff, World Airways, Air Carrier Service Corporation, Air Charter
Conversion to ATL-98	October 1960–June 1961
Rollout	June 17, 1961
First flight as ATL-98	June 21, 1961
Postmodification operators	British United Air Ferries, aircraft name "Golden Gate Bridge"
Scrapped in August 1970	

Carvair Two	c/n 10311-2
Original aircraft	Douglas C-54A-10-DC
Delivered to the US Army Air Force	May 27, 1944
USAAF serial	42-72206
Premodification operators	Federated Airlines, California Eastern Airways, Air Charter
Conversion to ATL-98	July 1961–March 1962
First flight as ATL-98	March 25, 1962
Postmodification operators	Channel Air Bridge, British United Air Ferries, British Air Ferries
Scrapped in August 1970	

Carvair Three	c/n 18339-3
Original aircraft	Douglas C-54B-5-DO
Delivered to the US Army Air Force	July 10, 1944
USAAF serial	43-17139
Premodification operators	Braniff, Northwest Orient, Transocean Airlines, Air Carrier Service Corporation
Conversion to ATL-98	July 1961–June 1962
First flight as ATL-98	June 28, 1962
Postmodification operators	Channel Air Bridge

Crashed while landing at Rotterdam on December 28, 1962. Capt. Tootill killed. The aircraft was written off.

Carvair Four	c/n 10338-4
Original aircraft	Douglas C-54A-10-DC
Delivered to the US Army Air Force	June 30, 1944
USAAF serial	42-72233
Premodification operators	Braniff, World Airways, Resort Airline, Slick Airways
Conversion to ATL-98	July 1961–September 1962
First flight as ATL-98	September 5, 1962
Postmodification operators	Intercontinental / Interocean / United Nations Organization ONUC, Compagnie Air Transport (CAT)

Destroyed in takeoff crash at Karachi on March 8, 1967. Four crew and seven people on the ground were killed.

Carvair Five	c/n 10365-5
Original aircraft	Douglas C-54A-15-DC
Delivered to the US Army Air Force	August 3, 1944
USAAF serial	42-72260
Premodification operators	US Navy as R5D-1 bureau number 50843, Veterans Air Express, Matson Airlines, Air Ceylon / Australian National Airlines, Twentieth Century Airlines / Seven Seas Airlines, Trans-Avia Flug / LTU, British United Airways
Conversion to ATL-98	December 1961–November 1962
First flight as ATL-98	November 2, 1962
Postmodification operators	Interocean, Compagnie Air Transport (CAT), Transports Aeriens Reunis / British Air Ferries, Pauling Middle East, UNI Air, Ruth May / Falcon Airways, Gifford Aviation / Kodiak Western Alaska Airlines (Air Fortynine), Custom Air Service

As N83FA, destroyed in takeoff crash on April 3, 1997. Crew of two killed.

Carvair Six	c/n 7480-6
Original aircraft	Douglas C-54A-5-DO
Delivered to the US Army Air Force	April 11, 1944
USAAF serial	42-107461
Premodification operators	American Airlines, Airplane Enterprises, AVENSA, Resort Airlines, World Airways
Conversion to ATL-98	June–October 1962
First flight as ATL-98	February 26, 1963
Postmodification operators	Aer Lingus, Eastern Provincial Airways

Written off after accident at Twin Falls, Labrador, on September 28, 1968

Carvair Seven	c/n 10273-7
Original aircraft	Douglas C-54A-1-DC
Delivered to the US Army Air Force	November 6, 1943
USAAF serial	42-72168
Premodification operators	California Eastern Airways, Transocean, Seaboard & Western
Conversion to ATL-98	August 1962–January 1963
First flight as ATL-98	March 19, 1963
Postmodification operators	British United Air Ferries (appeared in the James Bond movie *Goldfinger*), British Air Ferries, Invicta, Falcon Airways, Calm Air, Pacific Air Express / Kemavia Inc., Hondu Carib / Great Southern Airways, Great Arctic Airways

Written off after accident on June 28, 1997

Carvair Eight	c/n 10448-8
Original aircraft	Douglas C-54B-1-DC
Delivered to the US Army Air Force	November 15, 1944
USAAF serial	42-72343
Premodification operators	Twentieth Century Fox Airlines, North American Airlines, Resort Airlines, Slick Airways
Conversion to ATL-98	February–April 1963
First flight as ATL-98	April 18, 1963
Postmodification operators	Aer Lingus, Eastern Provincial Airways, British Air Ferries / Norwegian Overseas Airways

Cockpit section preserved

Carvair Nine	c/n 27249-9
Original aircraft	Douglas C-54B-20-DO
Delivered to the US Army Air Force	January 11, 1945
USAAF serial	44-9023

Douglas Aircraft Corporation purchased the aircraft in 1946 and converted the C-54 into a civil DC-4, which was given the registration NC88723

Premodification operators	Western Airlines, Guest Aerovias Mexico, Aerovias Panama Airways, Lloyd Aero Boliviano
Conversion to ATL-98	October 1962–June 1963
First flight as ATL-98	June 8, 1963
Postmodification operators	British Air Ferries, Falcon Airways, Nasco Leasing / Calm Air, Custom Air Service

Preserved in the autumn of 2021 with the registration N89FA; nicknamed "Fat Albert"

Carvair Ten	c/n 10382-10
Original aircraft	Douglas C-54A-15-DC
Delivered to the US Army Air Force	August 24, 1944
USAAF serial	42-72277
Premodification operators	Braathens S.A.F.E., Seaboard & Western, Trans Caribbean Airways, Interocean
Conversion to ATL-98	November 1962–July 1963
First flight as ATL-98	July 29, 1963
Postmodification operators	British United Air Ferries, Alisud, Air Ferry, CAT, Transports Aeriens Reunis, British Air Ferries, SOACO, Afrigo, EclAir
Destroyed in fighting in Kinshasa, Zaire, in September 1995	

Carvair Eleven	c/n 18333-11
Original aircraft	Douglas C-54B-5-DO
Delivered to the US Army Air Force	June 22, 1944
USAAF serial	43-17133
Premodification operators	Delta Air Lines, North American Airlines, Falcon Air, Blue Air
Conversion to ATL-98	December 1962–January 1965 (with lengthy pauses)
First flight as ATL-98	January 4, 1965
Postmodification operators	Air Ferry, British United Air Ferries, British Air Ferries
Scrapped at Le Touquet, France, after landing accident on March 18, 1971	

Carvair Twelve	c/n 12-10351
Original aircraft	Douglas C-54A-15-DC
Delivered to the US Army Air Force	July 15, 1944
USAAF serial	42-72246
Premodification operators	Pan American Airways, Alitalia, California Eastern Airways, Air Charter, British United Airways
Conversion to ATL-98	April 1963–February 1964
First flight as ATL-98	February 11, 1964
Postmodification operators	AVIACO, British United Air Ferries, SF Air, British Air Ferries
Scrapped at Southend in December 1983	

Carvair Thirteen	c/n 3058-13
Original aircraft	Douglas C-54-DO
Delivered to the US Army Air Force	February 8, 1943
USAAF serial	41-37272
Premodification operators	Eastern Air Lines, California Eastern Airways, Global Airways, California Automotive, Continentale Deutsche Luftreederei
Conversion to ATL-98	July–December 1963
First flight as ATL-98	February 8, 1964
Postmodification operators	British United Air Ferries, British Air Ferries, SOACO, AFRIGO
Scrapped at Brazzaville in May 1986	

Carvair Fourteen	c/n 10458-14
Original aircraft	Douglas C-54B-1-DC
Delivered to the US Army Air Force	November 27, 1944
USAAF serial	42-72423
Premodification operators	Western Airlines, Sobelair, Sabena, Continentale Deutsche Luftreederei
Conversion to ATL-98	July 1963–April 1964
First flight as ATL-98	April 17, 1964
Postmodification operators	Aer Lingus, Eastern Provincial Airways, British Air Ferries, Rorosfly Cargo, Red Cross
Probably scrapped in 1985	

Carvair Fifteen	c/n 10528-1
Original aircraft	Douglas C-54E-5-DO
Delivered to the US Army Air Force	April 5, 1945
USAAF serial	44-9085
Premodification operators	Pan American Airways, Trans Mediterranean Airways
Conversion to ATL-98	November 1963–October 1964, then parked for 2.5 years
First flight as ATL-98	March 23, 1966
Postmodification operators	British United, CAT, Shell Nigeria, Transport Aeriens Reunis
Probably scrapped in 1972	

Carvair Sixteen	c/n 10485-16
Original aircraft	Douglas C-54B-1-DC
Delivered to the US Army Air Force	December 23, 1944
USAAF serial	42-72380
Premodification operators	American Airlines, Iberia
Conversion to ATL-98	February–May 1964
First flight as ATL-98	June 4, 1964
Postmodification operators	Aviaco, Dominicana
Written off after an accident on June 22, 1969	

Carvair Seventeen	c/n 18342-17
Original aircraft	Douglas C-54B-5-DO
Delivered to the US Army Air Force	July 19, 1944
USAAF serial	43-17142
Premodification operators	United Air Lines, Transocean, Lufthansa (leased), Babb Company, Intercontinental Airways (leased)
Conversion to ATL-98	began in February 1964, followed by three years of storage
First flight as ATL-98	February 19, 1969
Postmodification operators	British Air Ferries, Secmafer / SF Air, Airtime / Aero Union / Kodiak Western Alaska Airlines, Pacific Air Express / Kemavia / Philippine Air Lines, Hondu Carib / Custom Air Service
Scrapped sometime after February 1993	

Carvair Eighteen	c/n 18340-18
Original aircraft	Douglas C-54B-5-DO
Delivered to the US Army Air Force	July 12, 1944
USAAF serial	43-17140
Premodification operators	American Airlines, Iberia
Conversion to ATL-98	November 1964–February 1965
First flight as ATL-98	March 12, 1965
Postmodification operators	AVIACO, Compania Dominicana de Aviacion. Pieces displayed as highlight of the Piano Bar in Santo Domingo.

Carvair Nineteen	c/n 42927-19
Original aircraft	Douglas DC-4-1009
Originally delivered to Svensk Interkontinental Lufttrafik AB (SILA)	May 17, 1946
Civil registration	SE-BBD
Premodification operators	SILA, SAS, Japan Airlines, Ansett
Conversion to ATL-98	May–September 1965
First flight as ATL-98	September 14, 1965
Postmodification operators	Ansett, South East Asia Air Transport, Air Cambodge
Probably scrapped in 1980	

	c/n 42994-0
Original aircraft	Douglas DC-4-1009
Delivered to Norwegian airline DNL	June 24, 1946
Premodification operators	DNL, SAS, Ansett
Conversion to ATL-98	June–October 1965
First flight as ATL-98	October 27, 1965
Postmodification operators	Ansett, Air Australia (Singapore), Seulawah–Mandala Air Service, Bayu Air / Air Express Australia, Dwen Automotive, Nationwide Air International, James Air, Air Cargo Panama, Turner Aviation Limited, Pacific Aerolift, Hawaii Pacific Air / Air Cargo Hawaii, Hawk Air, Brooks Fuel
Destroyed in a crash in Alaska on May 30, 2007	

Carvair Twenty-One	c/n 27314-21
Original aircraft	Douglas C-54E-5-DO
Delivered to US Army Air Force	April 7, 1945
USAAF serial	44-9088
Premodification operators	Pan American Airways, Japan Air Lines, Ansett MacRobertson Miller Airlines (leased)
Conversion to ATL-98	March–July 1968
First flight as ATL-98	July 12, 1968
Postmodification operators	Ansett, Air Australia (Singapore), Bayu Indonesian, Air Express Australia, Dwen Automotive, Nationwide Air, James Air, Air Cargo Panama, Turner Aviation / Pacific Aerolift, Gold Crown Aviation, Hawaii Pacific Air / Air Cargo Hawaii, Phoebus Apollo

Preserved at Johannesburg Rand Airport, South Africa

Climb-out of ATL-98 CF-EPW of Eastern Provincial Airways above the snow covered Canadian landscape. *Courtesy of David Johnston*

CHAPTER 5
THE BERLIN AIRLIFT

DOUGLAS C-54 "CANDY BOMBERS" SAVE BERLIN

The Berlin Airlift of 1948 and 1949 was one of the largest humanitarian aid operations ever carried out by air in human history. Immediately after the end of the Second World War, there was a deep ideological rift between the Soviet Union, on the one hand, and the victorious Western Allies, the United States, Great Britain, and France, on the other. The focus of these geopolitical power games was increasingly on Berlin, the symbolic former center of power of Nazi Germany. Before the war ended, the victorious powers of the Second World War agreed on a four-power joint occupation of the city. Although the Soviet Union made a verbal promise to allow the militaries of the Western powers free access through the Soviet Occupation Zone to their Berlin sectors, a document signed by all sides in November 1945 guaranteed only three air corridors.

One month before the total blockade, the Soviet Union had already provoked its erstwhile allies by obstructing land and rail transports to the city. As a result, the American military governor in Germany, Gen. Lucius D. Clay, decided to set up a small airlift to supply the US units stationed in Berlin, flying around 200 tons of material to Tempelhof between April 2 and 4, 1948. Then, on the night of June 23–24, 1948, things got serious for the 2.2 million West Berliners. The Soviets set up barricades blocking all road, rail, and ship traffic to the western sectors, which were also cut off from the power supplied from the Soviet Occupation Zone. In the search for the right response to the Soviet provocation, there was initially disagreement within the American administration. Withdrawal from Berlin was considered, as well as the military liberation of the city by means of an attack across the Soviet occupation zone. A central role was played by General Clay, who vehemently advocated that the Western Allies remain in Berlin and whose unbending attitude impressed President Truman. Anticipating what was to come, on June 25, Clay ordered the establishment of an airlift to supply the Allied forces and the population of Berlin. President Truman confirmed it three days later with his terse official statement: "We are in Berlin and there we stay. Full stop." The first supply flights, by Douglas C-47 "raisin bombers," began on June

A Douglas C-54 on approach to Berlin-Tempelhof during the Berlin Airlift. The American Skymasters delivered the bulk of the tonnage delivered by air to Berlin. To this day it remains the largest humanitarian airlift of all time. *Courtesy of Dr. John Provan*

Children bring gifts to thank the pilots of the airlift. *Courtesy of Dr. John Provan*

Coal for heating the power plants and the stoves in the flats was one of the most vital cargoes brought to Berlin from West Germany on the C-54s. *Courtesy of Dr. John Provan*

Col. (Ret.) Gail Halvorsen, born October 10, 1920, is gratefully remembered in the hearts of many Berliners. Himself a pilot in the US Air Force during the Berlin Air Lift of 1948–49, Halvorsen flew Douglas C-54 transport aircraft, delivering essential goods and food to the cutoff western zones of the German metropolis.

One day he met some German children, standing at the fence of Berlin-Tempelhof airfield, watching the endless stream of landing and departing aircraft. Looking at their faces, marked by war and hardship, Halvorsen spontaneously gave them two sticks of gum he had in his pockets. Since this was of course not enough for the many hungry souls, he made a promise: "I'll be back tomorrow and will drop candy and chocolate from my C-54 during the approach to Tempelhof." That evening, Halvorsen made the first little parachutes from handkerchiefs, hanging the sweet cargo beneath. The very next day he kept his promise. He greeted the kids by waggling the wings of his aircraft and let the parachutes fly. This was the start of Operation Little Vittles. In the following months, 23 tons of candy was collected by American school children, who attached each package to a little parachute made from a handkerchief. This precious freight was then sent by the US military to Rhein-Main Air Force Base in West Germany, where not only Halvorsen but all his fellow Air Force pilots took them on their flights. From then on, and for the rest of the airlift, candy "rained" down to the thrilled children of West Berlin, anxiously waiting for the sweets from the sky as they stood below the approach path to Tempelhof Airfield. Ever since, Halvorsen has been known as the "Candy Bomber." *Courtesy of Dr. John Provan*

With this drawing, the northern German town of Fassberg, as one of several bridgeheads of the airlift, sent greetings to the trapped population of West Berlin. The drawing shows Douglas C-54s. *Courtesy of Dr. John Provan*

Douglas C-54s and C-47s of the USAF wait at Wiesbaden in Hesse for their next flights to Berlin. *Courtesy of Dr. John Provan*

26, 1948. On the American side the C-47s were soon replaced by Douglas C-54 Skymasters. The Royal Air Force, on the other hand, used Handley Page Hastings and Avro Tudor and York transports to replace their Dakotas. At the height of the airlift, which the British called Operation Plainfare and the US military referred to as Operation Vittles, hundreds of American aircraft flew through the southern corridor every day, with fifteen-minute intervals between aircraft flying at the same speed and staggered at three different altitudes, carrying aid supplies to Berlin. In this way, the limited airspace in the narrow corridor could be optimally utilized, and at peak times it was possible for a C-54 to land at Tempelhof every three minutes. After a precisely calculated turnaround time of just forty-nine minutes, the C-54 crews returned to Frankfurt/Main or Wiesbaden via the central corridor, also in a one-way traffic flow. Since Britain could not send a unified fleet to Berlin, and the many types of aircraft flew at different speeds, the British developed a system in which each type of aircraft shared an altitude band—and the aircraft flew in controlled two-way traffic through the northern corridor to Berlin and back to the British zone.

On May 12, 1949, the USSR lifted the blockade of West Berlin after the governments of the United States, Great Britain, France, and the USSR had adopted a joint communiqué to end the blockade and the counterblockade of the Soviet occupation zone. Nevertheless, the airlift could not be stopped from one day to the next, since the city's food and fuel stocks first had to be replenished, which lasted until September of that year. The last official flight as part of the British Operation Plainfare took place on September 6, 1949, while the US Air Force ceremoniously ended Operation Vittles on September 30, 1949.

This photo of a lucky Berlin youngster who got hold of a bar of American chocolate from Operation Little Vittles is worth a thousand words. *Courtesy of Dr John Provan*

Gail Halvorsen holding one of his famous candy bomber parachutes. *Courtesy of Dr. John Provan*

THE DOUGLAS C-54
IN THE BERLIN AIRLIFT

Up to 224 Douglas C-54s of the American military formed the backbone of the Berlin Airlift in 1948–49. In addition to C-54s of the US Air Force, the Americans also mobilized R5Ds of the US Naval Air Transport Service (NATS). Airlines such as American Overseas Airlines (AOA), Alaska Airlines, Seaboard & Western, and Transocean Airlines also took part in the airlift with their DC-4s—either directly, or indirectly by delivering materials to the American military bases at Wiesbaden and Frankfurt/Main in West Germany. One of the reasons why private companies took part was that the American military was unable to provide the required transport capacity for the "Big Lift" as quickly as required. AOA, which was acquired by Pan American in 1950, was the first airline to commit its DC-4s, beginning flights to Berlin immediately after the start of the Soviet blockade on June 26, 1948. The airline had been operating a passenger service, the so-called Internal German Service, between Frankfurt/Main and Berlin-Tempelhof with its four-engine transports, and once the blockade began it increased its resources to six DC-4s and one DC-3.

OTHER AIRCRAFT TYPES OF THE BERLIN AIRLIFT

Avro 685 York	
Manufacturer	A. V. Roe & Company Ltd., Great Britain
Wingspan	102 ft.
Length	79 ft.
Height	17 ft.
Power plants	4 × Rolls-Royce Merlin 50
Cruise	185 mph
Payload	20,500 lbs.

Avro 691 Lancastrian	
Manufacturer	A. V. Roe & Company Ltd., Great Britain
Wingspan	102 ft.
Length	77 ft.
Height	20 ft.
Power plants	4 × Rolls-Royce Merlin XXIV
Cruise	185 mph
Payload	18,600 lbs.

Avro 688 Tudor 5	
Manufacturer	A. V. Roe & Company Ltd., Great Britain
Wingspan	120 ft.
Length	106 ft.
Height	24 ft.
Power plants	4 × Rolls-Royce Merlin 621
Cruise	185 mph
Payload	17,950 lbs.

Boeing 367 / C-97 Stratofreighter	
Manufacturer	Boeing Aircraft Company, Seattle, USA
Wingspan	141 ft.
Length	110 ft.
Height	33 ft.
Power plants	4 × Pratt & Whitney R-4360 Wasp Major
Cruise	200 mph
Payload	53,000 lbs.

Bristol 170 Freighter	
Manufacturer	Bristol Aeroplane Company, Filton, Great Britain
Wingspan	108 ft.
Length	68 ft.
Height	21 ft.
Power plants	2 × Bristol Hercules 734
Cruise	164 mph
Payload	8,700 lbs.

Douglas C-47 Dakota / Skytrain	
Manufacturer	Douglas Aircraft Co. Inc., Santa Monica, California, US
Wingspan	95 ft.
Length	65 ft.
Height	17 ft.
Power plants	2 × Wright Cyclone G-102-A/2
Cruise	150 mph
Payload	7,480 lbs.

Handley Page H.P. 67 Hastings	
Manufacturer	Handley Page, Radlett, Great Britain
Wingspan	113 ft.
Length	81 ft.
Height	22 ft.
Power plants	4 × Bristol Hercules 101
Cruise	291 mph
Payload	20,311 lbs.

Handley Page H.P. 70 Halton	
Manufacturer	Handley Page, Radlett, Great Britain
Wingspan	104 ft.
Length	74 ft.
Height	22 ft.
Power plants	4 × Bristol Hercules
Cruise	185 mph
Payload	15,500 lbs.

Short S.45 Solent	
Manufacturer	Short Brothers, Rochester, Great Britain
Wingspan	113 ft.
Length	85 ft.
Height	33 ft.
Power plants	4 × Bristol Hercules 637
Cruise	165 mph
Payload	9,800 lbs.

Other aircraft types, such as the Avro Lincoln, Consolidated B-24 Liberator, Douglas C-74 Globemaster I, Fairchild C-82 Packet, and Vickers VC.1 Viking, were also used in smaller numbers for secondary support flights.

Airlift Statistics	
Quantity of food flown into Berlin	538,025 tons
Quantity of coal flown into Berlin	1,586,556 tons
Quantity of fuel and military and other goods flown into Berlin	201,266 tons
Passengers transported to and from Berlin	228,454
Air miles flown	104,358,951
Flights by Allied aircraft	555,370

THE COST

Thirty-nine British citizens, thirty-one Americans, and eight Germans lost their lives in the Berlin Airlift.

CHAPTER 6
DOUGLAS BIG PROPS IN SERVICE AS AIR FORCE ONE

Jokingly referred to as the "Sacred Cow" due to its secretive status, the Douglas VC-54C established the tradition of presidential aircraft provided by the US Air Force that continues to this day. *Courtesy of the US Air Force*

IT BEGAN WITH THE "SACRED COW"

In 1944, the first aircraft of the American armed forces reserved exclusively for the transport of an American president took to the air. Jokingly referred to as the "Sacred Cow" due to its secretive status, the Douglas VC-54C established the tradition of presidential aircraft provided by the United States Air Force that continues to this day. Franklin D. Roosevelt was the first sitting American president to use an aircraft for his travels, in 1943. It must be remembered that these were the pioneering years of aviation, and flying was an adventure with an uncertain outcome compared to today. Regardless, Roosevelt entrusted himself to the Boeing 314 flying boat "Dixie Clipper," officially owned by the US Navy and flown by a civilian crew from Pan American World Airways. The premier flight took him to the secret meeting with British prime minister Churchill in Casablanca, Morocco. After the success of this first flight, the US administration decided that the US Army Air Force (USAAF) should provide aircraft and crew for the air transport of the commander in chief. This led to the order of a comfortably appointed Consolidated C-87 transport aircraft, a civil version of the

The "Sacred Cow" served both President Roosevelt and his successor, Harry S. Truman. *Courtesy of the US Air Force*

The cockpit of the VC-54C has been preserved in perfect condition to this day. *Courtesy of the US Air Force*

On July 26, 1947, Truman signed the National Security Act, which took effect on September 18 of that year, on board the aircraft. Among its provisions was the creation of the US Air Force. The "Sacred Cow" was thus the birthplace of the American air force as an independent branch of the armed services. *Courtesy of the US Air Force*

B-24 Liberator bomber. However, after the US Secret Service raised security concerns, Gen. "Hap" Arnold, commander in chief of the USAAF, decided to order a more reliable VC-54C, specially equipped for presidential transport, from Douglas as an alternative. Officially designated "the Flying White House," it is still better known today as the "Sacred Cow," since its VIP equipment and use were initially shrouded in secrecy. To give it greater range, the fuselage of a standard C-54A was combined with the wings of a C-54B and its larger fuel tanks. The "Sacred Cow" served both President Roosevelt and his successor Harry S. Truman. For the wheelchair-bound Roosevelt, a battery-operated lift was specially built into the fuselage, with the help of which the president reached the cabin from the apron. A highlight was Roosevelt's flight in February 1945 aboard this VC-54C to the Yalta Conference, where the Allies decided on the division of postwar Germany. On July 26, 1947, Truman signed the National Security Act on board this aircraft, which came into force on September 18 of that year—and included the decision to establish the US Air Force. The "Sacred Cow" is thus considered the birthplace of the American air force as an independent branch of the armed forces. The four-engined presidential aircraft "Columbine II," a Lockheed VC-121A, and "Columbine III," a VC-121E, both of which have also been preserved, were also legendary. While the smaller VC-121A Constellation will continue to enrich the American vintage aviation scene in the future, the VC-121E Super Constellation "Columbine III," like many of its successors, is part of the exhibition at the National Museum of the US Air Force, located at Wright-Patterson Air Force Base near Dayton, Ohio.

The same is true of one of the two surviving Douglas VC-118s, which Truman named in honor of his hometown of Independence, Missouri. It was the direct successor to the "Sacred Cow" and the twenty-ninth aircraft produced in the Douglas DC-6 series. President Harry S. Truman used it as Air Force One between 1947 and 1953. The VC-118 differed from the commercial aircraft of the same type by having a presidential stateroom in the rear of the aircraft and a comfortably furnished main cabin for just

The metal fuselage of the VC-54C still shines as if brand new. *Courtesy of the US Air Force*

For the wheelchair-bound President Roosevelt, a battery-operated lift was specially installed in the fuselage, with the help of which the president reached the cabin from the apron. *Courtesy of the US Air Force*

The Douglas VC-118 of the National Museum of the US Air Force was christened by President Truman in honor of his hometown of Independence, Missouri. It was the direct successor to the "Sacred Cow" and the twenty-ninth aircraft of the Douglas DC-6 series to be produced. *Courtesy of the US Air Force*

The VC-118 differed from the commercial aircraft of the same type in that it featured technical improvements, a presidential stateroom in the rear of the aircraft, and a comfortably furnished main cabin for a maximum of twenty-four passengers on daytime flights. *Courtesy of the US Air Force / Ken LaRock*

twenty-four passengers on day flights, which could be converted into twelve "berths" for night flights. Other technical modifications included reversible-pitch propellers, a weather radar, a radar altimeter, an autopilot, and additional instrumentation improved over the standard civilian DC-6. Water injection gave the Pratt & Whitney piston engines increased takeoff power, and larger fuel tanks allowed the aircraft to reach any destination in the US from Washington, DC, nonstop. The striking appearance of the "Independence" when it was officially launched on Independence Day in 1947 was based on a suggestion by the Douglas Aircraft Company. Its first mission took President Truman to an international conference in the Brazilian metropolis of Rio de Janeiro on August 31 of that year. One of the most important flights in US history, however, was Truman's trip to Wake Island in October 1950, where he discussed the state of the Korean War with General Douglas MacArthur, commander in chief of the United Nations Peacekeeping Forces. The "Independence" was decommissioned in May 1953 after six years of service with the White House and continued to operate as a VIP aircraft for various units of the US Air Force. Transferred to the US Air Force Museum as an exhibit in 1965, it was restored to its original condition and livery by museum staff in 1977 and 1978.

The second VC-118, based on the civil Douglas DC-6, can be found in the Pima Air Museum, near Tucson, Arizona. It bears the registration 53-3240 and was operated by the 1254th Air Transport (Special Missions) Wing, stationed at Andrews Air Force Base in Maryland. It was a grand finale to the era of piston-powered presidential aircraft. It served Presidents Kennedy and Johnson only occasionally on trips abroad as the official Air Force One, because with the parallel introduction of the four-engine VC-137C long-range jet based on the Boeing 707-320B, this was usually the first choice. But the VC-118 that is on display in the Pima Air Museum was regularly used from 1962 onward for flights to smaller airports—where the VC-137C could not land—or as a replacement aircraft for the larger jet.

Since 1990, the most powerful man in the world has traveled on one of two VC-25As at his disposal. The aircraft, based on the Boeing 747-200, with the serial numbers 92-9000 and 82-8000, look completely identical, and both are parked next to each other, ready for takeoff when the president sets off on a trip. For security reasons, it is not decided until immediately before takeoff which of the two aircraft the president of the United States will be flying on—and which of the two aircraft will only then officially mutate into Air Force One. If the president is not on board one of the two VC-25As, the call sign of this aircraft changes to either SAM 28000 or SAM 29000. The fact that the call sign can also change to Air Force One during the flight is proven by the return transport of President John F. Kennedy, who was assassinated in Dallas, to Washington, DC, on November 22, 1963. The flight took off as SAM 2600 but landed in the American capital as Air Force One after Vice President Lyndon B. Johnson was sworn in on board as the new US president. Should an American president travel on an Army, Navy, or Coast Guard plane or helicopter, this flight will be given the radio call sign Army One, Navy One, Marine One, or Coast Guard One, analogous to the jets of the Air Force. Even an Executive One is conceivable, should the president use an aircraft with a US civil registration. The latter call sign has also been used for the departure of an outgoing president when he leaves the White House by naval helicopter on the day of the handover to his successor. Incidentally, the tradition of the Air Force One call sign did not begin with the "Sacred Cow" of 1944, but nine years later, and it became known worldwide only through the intensive travel diplomacy of the legendary US president John F. Kennedy and his VC-137C jets used in 1962 and 1963. The reason for the renaming of the presidential call sign was an incident in 1953, when "Columbine II," with President Dwight D. Eisenhower on board and the assigned call sign Air Force 8610, almost collided in the air with the passenger flight Eastern Air Lines 8610 because the call signs were confused in radio communication.

Perhaps the most historically important and internationally best-known Air Force One is the VC-137C, delivered

Another VC-118 can be found in the Pima Air Museum, near Tucson, Arizona. It bears the serial 53-3240 and was operated by the 1254th Air Transport (Special Missions) Wing, stationed at Andrews Air Force Base in Maryland. *Courtesy of John Bezosky, Pima Air and Space Museum*

on October 10, 1962, with the serial 62-6000 and the call sign SAM Two-Six-Thousand. In addition to Kennedy, this aircraft also served the seven presidents who followed him: Johnson, Nixon, Ford, Carter, Reagan, George H. W. Bush, and Clinton. In June 1963, John F. Kennedy flew aboard SAM 26000 to West Berlin to deliver his famous "Ich bin ein Berliner" speech. In November of that year, he departed with her on the fateful trip to Dallas. Whether it was President Johnson's flights to Southeast Asia during the Vietnam War or the first visit by an American president to China in February 1972, when Nixon met Mao Zedong—SAM 26000 was always the reliable Air Force One. In October 1981, the aircraft carried three former US presidents—Nixon, Ford, and Carter—to the funeral of the assassinated Egyptian president Anwar el-Sadat. And even Queen Elizabeth II used SAM 26000 in March 1983 during her state visit to the United States. Although this jet faded into the background somewhat with the acquisition of a newer VC-137C (72-7000) in December 1972, it remained in service until May 1998 as the Air Force One replacement aircraft, for transporting the vice president as well as high-ranking government officials. Accordingly, the handover of this aircraft, so important for the history of the United States, to the Museum of the US Air Force was broadcast live on American television—since it was the farewell of an active member of the government into a well-deserved retirement.

Less in the spotlight of the press were the no-less-important smaller aircraft types that also belonged to the presidential fleet over the decades. Among them was the four-engine Lockheed L-1329 (VC-140B) JetStar, which was at its peak at the time of Lyndon B. Johnson's presidency. Other jets and propeller-driven types included the North American T-39A Sabreliner, Aero Commander 500 (L-26 and U-4B), Beech VC-6A, Gulfstream Aerospace C-20B, and Bell UH-13J Sioux helicopter.

The VC-25As based on the Boeing 747-200 Jumbo Jet, which are current at the time of writing, are used by the Presidential Airlift Group assigned to the 89th Airlift Wing of the Air Mobility Command, stationed at Joint Base Andrews. Like "the Flying White House" of 1944, the interior of the VC-25A is designed like a flying official residence of the incumbent president. On board are a communications center, meeting rooms, a medical facility, a kitchen, an area for security personnel and government guests as well as representatives of the press—and of course the presidential office. However, the days of the two current presidential aircraft are numbered, since the conversion of two secondhand 747-85Ms into VC-25Bs began at Boeing's San Antonio plant in Texas on February 25, 2020. A piquant detail is that the two selected jets were originally ordered by the Russian airline Transaero, which has been insolvent since 2015, but were not accepted. As a result, for years the Jumbos sat mothballed in the aircraft graveyard at Victorville, California.

CHAPTER 7
SAS'S FLYING VIKING LONGSHIPS

MAIDEN FLIGHT TO NEW YORK

On August 1, 1946, the largest airlines in Denmark, Norway, and Sweden merged to form the Scandinavian Airlines System (SAS). However, the original cooperation agreement among the Danish Det Danske Luftfartselskab A/S (DDL), the Norwegian Det Norske Luftfartselkap A/S (DNL), and the two Swedish airlines, Svensk Interkontinental Lufttrafik AB (SILA) and AB Aerotransport (ABA), was initially limited to intercontinental air traffic to North and South America. This first Overseas SAS (OSAS) was followed by the consolidation of European flights into the European SAS (ESAS) on May 14, 1948. It was not until October 1951 that the Scandinavian "United Nations of the Skies" was expanded to include all commercial activities under the common brand name SAS. Initially, ten Douglas DC-4s were used on long-haul flights, the purchase contract for which had been signed between SILA president Per A. Norlin and the Douglas Aircraft Company on November 25, 1943, in the middle of the Second World War. By then, Denmark and Norway were occupied by Nazi Germany, and Sweden, neutral on paper, feared suffering the same fate.

Amid these dangerous times, Norlin was in the United States to finalize the order for the Douglas DC-4. His optimism in this matter, which seems strange to many, was not unfounded, because the year 1943 is considered the turning point of the Second World War. Not only did this year see the German army suffer defeats at Stalingrad and El Alamein; moreover, the Western Allies Great Britain and the United States decided at the Casablanca Conference on January 21 of that year to launch a combined bomber offensive against the German Reich to break the morale of the population. Only six days later, the first Boeing B-17s of the US Army Air Force took off from Great Britain to attack Wilhelmshaven. While a relentless air war raged over the Third Reich and the occupied neighboring countries, and many people lost their lives as cities were reduced to rubble, peace and quiet outwardly prevailed in neutral Sweden. In reality, the Swedish government officially pursued a policy of neutrality but acted in a decidedly opportunistic manner toward Germany to protect its own country, especially in the first half of the war. It was not until the summer of 1943 that Sweden increasingly turned economically and politically toward the Western Allies. This change

The DC-4 "Dan Viking" over the skyscrapers of Manhattan while on its maiden flight from Scandinavia to New York. *Courtesy of SAS*

The Swedish airline SILA established the first commercial air link between the USA and Europe after the end of the Second World War, using a Boeing B-17 Flying Fortress converted into a passenger aircraft. *Courtesy of SAAB*

This first flight cover was transported on board the SILA Boeing B-17 "Felix" premier flight from Stockholm to New York. *Author's collection*

in policy was expressed not least in the founding of the airline Svensk Interkontinental Lufttrafik AB. To avoid diplomatic complications, it was founded in close cooperation with the state-owned AB Aerotransport (ABA), but by private investors. After all, its primary task was to prepare for postwar air traffic to the United States. SILA director Per A. Norlin was in the midst of negotiations in the US for traffic rights and export licenses for the intended Douglas purchase when news reached him on July 24, 1943, of the first emergency landing by an American Flying Fortress in his native Sweden. The Boeing B-17F "Georgia Rebel" belonged to the 535th Bombardment Squadron of the 381st Bombardment Group. Its ten-man crew, under the command of 1Lt. O. V. Jones, was involved in an attack on a factory in Heröya, Norway, near Ålesund, when their B-17 was damaged by German defensive fire. This caused one engine to fail completely, while a second failed to produce full power. Damaged in this way, a return to its base in Britain was out of the question—and so the crew decided to fly on to neutral and therefore safe Sweden. There, after a flight time of about fourteen hours, the "Georgia Rebel" made a belly landing near the village of Vännacka. ABA boss Carl Florman and his team recognized the opportunity presented by the emergency landing by the American bomber to establish a secure courier service to Great Britain and possibly as far as Moscow with suitably converted Flying Fortresses. Immediately after the "Georgia Rebel's" landing, therefore, Florman sent the head of his engineering department, Karl Lignell, with a team of experts to Vännacka. They examined the B-17 in detail and deemed it suitable for repair.

In close coordination with ABA's Florman and the Swedish embassy in the United States, Norlin personally negotiated with the commander in chief of the American air force, Gen. H. H. "Hap" Arnold, in Washington, DC, in the winter of 1943 about the possibility of converting the "Georgia Rebel" and other B-17s that had since landed in Sweden into courier aircraft for the transport of spies, industrialists, and military personnel, as well as for strategic products produced in Sweden, such as ball bearings. This idea resulted in a kind of horse-trading deal that involved the loan of ten B-17s to Sweden in exchange for three hundred interned American crew members from bombers that had made forced landings. At the end of the war, Gen. Arnold said, the Swedish state could then formally acquire the aircraft for the symbolic price of one dollar each. Operation Felix was able to get underway—and two B-17Fs and five B-17 Gs were converted into civil airliners at the SAAB Aircraft Works in Linköping. Two more B-17Fs and parts of a third aircraft, including the "Georgia Rebel," served as sources of spare parts. Three aircraft flew officially for SILA, while two were used by ABA. Two more B-17s were kept for the Danish DDL, which began using them in the summer of 1945. Before they were used as civilian courier aircraft, SAAB technicians removed all military equipment. In place of the bomber's glazed nose, they installed a new nose section, extended by 3.3 feet, in which cargo and navigation compartments were installed. The former bomb bays also became cargo holds, while in the aft section of the fuselage, two passenger cabins offered relatively comfortable accommodations. There was also a lavatory and an unarmed observation position in the tail, formerly the tail gunner's position. Up to fourteen passengers could be accommodated aboard the civil B-17.

These Felix aircraft were named after the US Air Force attaché in Sweden, Felix M. Hardison. In this capacity, not only was he closely involved in the negotiations for the loan of the ten bombers to the Swedish state, but as a former B-17 pilot he was also intimately involved in the flight training of the Swedish crews. In gratitude for this, not only were the civil Boeings converted by SAAB officially designated B-17 Felix, but the courier flights flown by them were also dubbed Operation Felix. The first flight to Scotland was made by aircraft SE-BAH "Sam" under the command of Capt. Marshall Lindholm on October 9, 1944. It took off from Stockholm-Bromma at exactly 4:15 p.m. and first set course north over Swedish territory before flying west, crossing Norway north of Trondheim and heading south along the Shetland Islands to Prestwick. Once there, Scottish Aviation took care of the technical aspects of the aircraft while BOAC handled the passengers and cargo. The calculation had worked. Not a single Boeing was lost on these courier flights, and none of its crew members or even a single passenger was injured or killed during Operation Felix, which continued until the end of the war.

With the end of the Second World War in Europe, these courier flights became unnecessary. But this did not mean that the four-engined B-17 long-haul aircraft were old-fashioned. In fact, SILA used its Flying Fortresses to open the first passenger route across the North Atlantic just seven weeks after the end of the war, prior to delivery of the DC-4s ordered in 1943. On the basis of the air transport agreement between Sweden and the United States negotiated by Per A. Norlin in 1943, the first flight was able to take off as early as June 27, 1945, from Stockholm-Bromma via Reykjavik, Iceland, and the Canadian Mingan Archipelago toward New York–La Guardia. Registered SE-BAK and christened "Jim," the B-17F with the construction number 5775 rewrote aviation history with this flight. A worthy task for the former bomber, which originally flew as "Veni Vidi Vici" ("I came, I saw, I conquered"). The last Felix B-17 used by ABA and SILA, with the registration SE-BAN and christened "Ted," carried passengers from Cairo, Egypt, to its base in Stockholm-Bromma on August 7, 1947, where it was scrapped in 1948. Together, the seven Swedish Felix B-17s flew 1,454,008 miles as passenger aircraft, flying regularly scheduled services even from Stockholm to Rio de Janeiro! Two B-17 Felix aircraft were sold to Denmark after the end of the war and were used with the registrations OY-DFA and OY-DFE on passenger flights of the Danish airline DDL within Europe as well as on the long-haul route to Johannesburg, South Africa. After the aircraft with construction number 21982 and the registration OY-DFE had to be written off on January 30, 1946, as a result of an accident, the former B-17G "Shoo Shoo Baby" of the US Army Air Force remained in airline service as the last example of the Swedish conversion series. It was not until 1948 that it changed hands and went to the Danish air force as "Store Bjørn" ("Big Bear") with the new serial 67-672. Many other stations followed before the

Scandinavian
SAS
SCANDINAVIAN AIRLINES SYSTEM
SK-
SAS

by-then-badly-damaged aircraft was able to take to the air again at Dover Air Force Base, Delaware, after a comprehensive restoration in the United States by volunteers of the 512th Antique Aircraft Restoration Group. On October 15, 1988, the veteran aircraft, which had been restored to its original condition as a 1944 B-17G, took off on its second maiden flight. The destination was the airfield of the US Air Force Museum at Wright-Patterson Air Force Base. This was the second time in forty-four years that aircraft number 42-32076 had landed at the same airbase where it had stopped on its delivery flight to Bassingbourn Air Force Base in 1944.

With the end of operations by the Felix B-17s, the Scandinavian DC-4s began joining the fleet. All ten Douglas DC-4-1009s arrived in May and June 1946 at Copenhagen (two), Oslo (two), and Stockholm (six) for use by DDL, DNL, ABA, and SILA. After initially flying under the names and logos of the four airlines, following the formation of SAS the aircraft were gradually painted in SAS's distinctive design of a historic Viking ship. Formally, however, they remained with the founding airlines of the still-young SAS consortium until February 8, 1951.

At that time, premier flights with brand-new Douglas DC-4s and the approximately five hundred C-54 and R5D aircraft "civilianized" from army stocks were taking place around the globe. But few of these premieres are as well documented as that of the first SAS transatlantic crossing from Scandinavia to the "Big Apple." The DC-4 left Stockholm-Bromma on September 17, 1946, and reached New York–La Guardia after stopovers in Copenhagen, Prestwick in Scotland, and Gander, Newfoundland. With the DC-4 "Dan Viking," SAS also established its tradition, still maintained today, of naming each of its aircraft after famous Nordic queens and kings as well as heroic figures from the Viking era.

The premiere did not go quite as planned for the twenty-eight guests of honor invited by SAS, since shortly after takeoff in Copenhagen there were technical problems, and Flight Captain Byron S. Cramblet decided to turn back for safety's sake. However, this did not stop the illustrious

An SAS DC-4 flies over New York's Statue of Liberty, which means that it will soon reach its destination, New York's La Guardia Airport. *Courtesy of SAS Museum, Oslo*

Before the actual premier flight, SAS flew Scandinavian press representatives to New York to report on the arrival of the "Dan Viking" and the subsequent celebrations. *Courtesy of SAS Museum, Oslo*

crowd of guests from moving the merry party that had begun on board to the center of Copenhagen until "Dan Viking" was ready for takeoff again eight hours later. This time all went well, even if the crew forgot to take down the two SAS flags proudly flying above the cockpit before takeoff, which were soon reduced to tatters on their poles. This was by no means Cramblet's first Atlantic crossing at the controls of an aircraft, since the American had already been regularly deployed on USAAF ferry flights in the last two years of the Second World War. After the war ended, he applied to ABA in Sweden and took part in numerous SAS training flights between Scandinavia and the United States before the big premiere. Cramblet remained with SAS until 1948, when he reenlisted in the US Air Force and flew Douglas C-54s in the Berlin Airlift in 1948–49.

Strictly speaking, SAS celebrated not one but two premieres. On August 5, 1946, a SILA DC-4 with an SAS flight number took off from Stockholm for the United States. However, since the airline had been founded only five days earlier, there was no time to repaint the Douglas airliner. So, strictly speaking, September 17 was the first transatlantic flight of a DC-4 in full SAS livery, followed by the first flight

The flight crew were also invited to the grand gala evening at the Waldorf Astoria Hotel celebrating the first landing by an SAS DC-4 at New York. *Courtesy of SAS Museum, Oslo*

This dramatic in-flight photograph shows the Douglas DC-4 in its element. *Courtesy of SAS Museum, Oslo*

BOEING
Stratocruiser
SVENSK INTERKONTINENTAL
LUFTTRAFIK AB
STOCKHOLM-SWEDEN
SE-BBH
SWEDISH AIR LINES
SILA
SE-
BBH

AIRLINES SYSTEM
TORKIL VIKING
238

in the opposite direction from New York on September 18 with twenty-eight invited American guests. In addition to the SAS top management and the heads of the four SAS founding airlines, Prince Axel of Denmark and ministers of the three Scandinavian nations involved, as well as various diplomats, were on board on the flight from Stockholm. A day earlier, a special SAS flight had landed at La Guardia with twenty-eight Scandinavian press representatives, who documented this premiere photographically and with their reports, while another special flight filled with American journalists took off for the weeklong round trip to Scandinavia at the invitation of SAS.

After "Dan Viking" had arrived at La Guardia Airport's Marine Air Terminal after about twenty-eight hours on September 18, 1946, the guests of honor had a day to recover before a large inaugural banquet with three hundred guests in the Grand Ballroom of the Waldorf Astoria. The main speaker at the various addresses was Fiorello La Guardia, former mayor of New York and at that time chairman of the United Nations Relief and Rehabilitation Administration (UNRRA). Only shortly before, the destination airport of the SAS premier flight had been named after him. He was followed on the list of speakers by Trygve Lie, Norwegian director general of the United Nations, as well as Thomas F. J. Corcoran, deputy mayor of New York, and Per Kampmann, chairman of the board of directors of SAS. Dr. Henry Goddard Leach, president of the American-Scandinavian Foundation, concluded the illustrious lineup of speakers as toastmaster.

When it launched the new route, SAS offered two weekly flights between New York and Scandinavia, alternating via Oslo or Copenhagen to Stockholm-Bromma. On the occasion of the premier flight, SAS also announced that it would be introducing the Boeing 377 Stratocruiser into service in 1947. With its higher cruising speed and greater range, the Boeing airliner was supposed to halve the time en route from around twenty-eight to fourteen hours. In fact, Scandinavian Airlines System had taken an order from Swedish Intercontinental Airlines for four aircraft, designated Boeing 377-10-28. A historical drawing commemorates SILA as the original fifth Boeing customer. As early as 1945, engineers from the Swedish AB Aerotransport (ABA), commissioned by SILA, examined the key economic data of the first Boeing 377 designs. They compared them with the competing Douglas DC-4 and DC-6, as well as the Lockheed L-049 and the never-built Lockheed L-549. Their conclusion: the operating costs of the Boeing 377 were considerably lower than those of the competing designs. Encouraged by these figures, SILA ordered four Stratocruisers on February 26, 1946, half a year before the merger into SAS, for delivery the following year. However, delivery delays at Boeing and SAS's desire for a homogeneous Douglas fleet led to a search for a buyer for the unwanted Stratocruisers. In May 1949, the British airline BOAC finally agreed to take over the delivery positions of the aircraft, due for delivery in June and August of that year. Since it was already too late at that time to adapt the aircraft to BOAC standards, the SILA/SAS Boeing 377-10-28s differed in some points from the six other 377-10-32s operated by BOAC. For example, the galley was in the rear of the Stratocruiser—in contrast to its central location in the other aircraft. There were further differences in various details of the cabin equipment, including the color of the seat upholstery and the cockpit instrumentation. Externally, the two BOAC variants differed in the shape of the cabin windows in the lower deck. As with the choice of a galley position in the middle of the fuselage or in the rear, the airlines had the option to choose between rectangular or circular cabin windows. Thus, Stratocruisers flew exclusively

SILA, the Swedish partner in SAS, had ordered four Boeing 377 Stratocruisers in 1946. However, delays in delivery of the Boeings and the reliability of the Douglas DC-4 and DC-6 led SAS to pass this order on to the British airline BOAC. *Courtesy of Boeing*

The Douglas DC-6B Cloudmaster was used on the entire SAS long-haul network and proved to be an outstanding success. *Courtesy of SAS*

with round windows on both decks, as with Pan American Airways and BOAC's ex-SILA aircraft, or exclusively rectangular windows, as with Northwest Orient, or a combination of both—rectangular windows above and round windows in the lower deck, as with United, or round windows above and rectangular windows below, as with American Overseas Airways (AOA) and BOAC.

SAS, on the other hand, built its long-haul fleet around its Douglas four-engined, propeller-driven airliners. The DC-4 Skymaster of 1946 was followed two years later by the first DC-6 Cloudmaster, in 1952 by the DC-6B, and finally in 1956 by the Douglas DC-7C Seven Seas. From the time of its foundation, SAS remained loyal to Douglas and McDonnell Douglas as the preferred supplier of its aircraft fleet for decades. DC-4, DC-6, DC-6B, DC-7C, DC-8-32, DC-8-55, DC-8-62, DC-8-63, DC-9-21, DC-9-33AF, DC-9-41, DC-9-81, DC-10-30, MD-81, MD-82, MD-83, MD-87, MD-90-30—the list of aircraft types delivered from the factory reads like the almost complete sales catalog of the traditional company. In addition, DC-3s, DC-9-51s, DC-10-10s, and MD-95s were acquired second-hand, rounding off the picture of SAS as one of the most loyal Douglas customers.

Conscientious maintenance, as on this DC-6B, was then as now one of the cornerstones of safe flight operations. *Courtesy of Harald Borgmann*

In the 1950s, there were no video screens in the cabin where passengers could follow the flight from their seats. This was more than made up for by personal service from the cabin crew. *Courtesy of SAS / author's archive*

The tail of a DC-6 adorns this SAS brochure from the late 1940s. *Courtesy of SAS / author's archive*

The Viking motif was used again and again by SAS for advertising until the 1980s, as on this route map from January 1950. *Courtesy of SAS / author's archive*

SCANDINAVIAN
SAS
- for speed and service

SCANDINAVIAN AIRLINES SYSTEM
ROUTEMAP
This routemap covers our winter
program. — Local timetables are
issued in most countries, and are
easily recognized by the cover
with the three Scandinavian flags
Issued January 15,
1950

Unlike today, Hamburg airport in northern Germany was a hub for SAS long-haul traffic. Provided with the appropriate traffic rights, the Scandinavian airline flew from Germany to the US, South America, and Asia. *Courtesy of Hamburg airport*

Since air travel was something very special and very expensive, passengers were treated accordingly. This included being symbolically named "Vikings of the Air" by SAS and the presentation of a certificate to that effect. *Courtesy of SAS / author's archive*

To give the passengers some idea of where the aircraft would be during the journey and the anticipated time of arrival, the captain would fill out a "flight report" like this one. It was passed from one row of seats to the next—until each of the guests had studied it. *Courtesy of SAS / author's archive*

This promotional postcard from the late 1940s revealed where one could travel around the world on an SAS DC-6. *Courtesy of SAS / author's archive*

Delicious "Royal Viking Service" on board a SAS Douglas propliner. *Courtesy of SAS Museum, Oslo*

CHAPTER 8

THE SAS POLAR EXPRESS

FIRST OVER THE POLE

Around a thousand years ago, a small Viking boat under the command of Leif Eriksson set sail from the coast of Greenland. Her courageous crew of thirty-six set out to explore the unknown sea beyond the mighty icebergs—and discovered America by chance. Five hundred years before Christopher Columbus, Scandinavians had already established a colony in the New World. In the style of their ancestors, in the 1950s the "flying Vikings" of the modern era sought safe ways to traverse the ice deserts of the Arctic. With the two Norwegian polar pioneers Bernt Balchen and Hjalmar Riiser-Larsen in their ranks, men who had taken part in polar expeditions by plane and airship in the 1920s, SAS created new twentieth-century trade routes among Europe, Asia, and North America.

The conquest of the Arctic Ocean was a challenge that a Venetian navigator in British service took on for the first time in 1496. Just two years after Christopher Columbus, who initially discovered not America but only one of the Bermuda Islands, Giovanni Caboto set sail from the British city of Bristol on a northwesterly course and reached Labrador, now part of the Canadian province of Newfoundland. So, to the Venetian goes the honor of being the first European of modern times to have landed on the North American continent. Henry Hudson, who first succeeded in crossing Hudson Straight, which was named after him, in the Arctic in 1610, and Martin Frobisher, discoverer and namesake of Frobisher Bay, were other British seafarers who sought a sea route from the Atlantic across the polar region to the Pacific—the so-called Northwest Passage. It was not until 1903, however, that the Norwegian polar explorer Roald Amundsen succeeded in doing so, reaching Nome, Alaska, with his ship *Gjøa* after a three-year journey. But it was not just the sea route through the Arctic that fascinated people at the time, but also the race to the North Pole. The first to reach the North Pole was the American commodore Robert Edwin Peary and his team on April 6, 1909—after twenty-three years of intensive preparations, during which he proved, among other things, that Greenland is an island. After Peary achieved his triumph with the help of dogsled teams, Adm. Richard E. Byrd and Floyd Bennett took off from Spitsbergen on May 9, 1926, for the first flight over the North Pole. Their flight time was fifteen hours and thirty minutes. Only three days later, Roald

LOS-ANGELES
CITY LIMIT
SAS

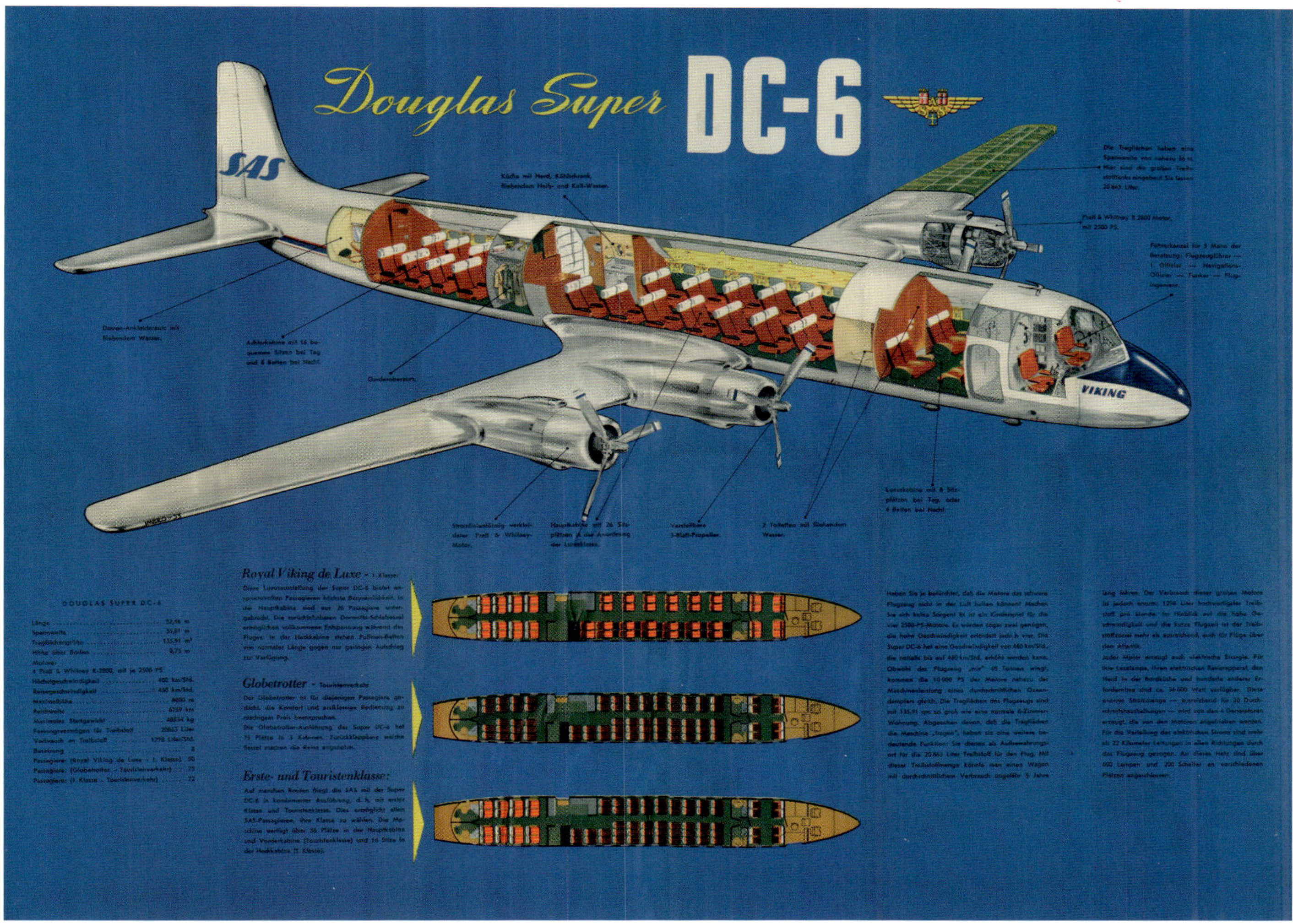

On the occasion of the ceremonial inauguration of the SAS polar shortcut between Copenhagen and Los Angeles on November 15, 1954, the mayor of Los Angeles, Norris Poulsen, raised the symbolic "Los-Angeles City Limit" sign at the Danish capital's airport. *Courtesy of SAS*

The Douglas DC-6Bs, called "Douglas Super DC-6s" by SAS, were used in three configurations, as can be seen on this contemporaneous leaflet: "Royal Viking de Luxe," first class; "Globetrotter," tourist class; and a mixed version with first class in the rear and tourist class in the noisier forward cabin area. *Courtesy of SAS / author's collection*

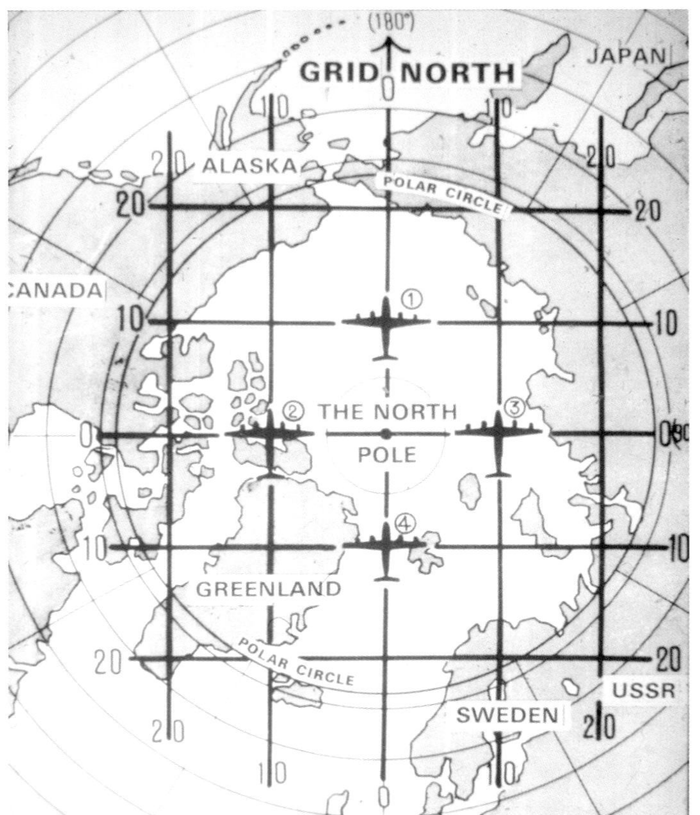

SAS navigators used the Polar Grid Chart developed by the airline to determine their position over the Arctic. These grids replaced the conventional division into degrees of longitude and latitude, which, as an aircraft approaches the North Pole, it passes at increasingly shorter intervals until there is only one possible heading: south. *Courtesy of SAS / author's collection*

At the heart of the orange-sized Polar Path gyroscopic compass was a gyro that stabilized itself at 23,000 revolutions per minute. Like a humming top for children, the electrically driven instrument maintained its position in space—and reliably kept the machine's autopilot on course. *Courtesy of SAS / author's collection*

The DC-7C, christened the Global Express by SAS, enabled commercial air traffic for the first time on what was then the shortest route between Europe and Japan, via the North Pole with a stopover in Alaska. *Courtesy of SAS / author's collection*

safety
on board
SCANDINAVIAN AIRLINES SYSTEM
DENMARK   NORWAY   SWEDEN
Emergency Exit - Nødutgang
Notausgang   - Salida de emergencia
DC7C
DC6B
DC6
METROPOLITAN
SCANDIA
DC3

In the 1950s, safety cards were generally valid for several aircraft types and were not as detailed as they are today. There were only a few safety cards specific to a single aircraft type. This is illustrated by this safety card from SAS, which was valid for the airline's entire fleet. This included the Douglas DC-6, DC-6B, and DC-7C. *Courtesy of SAS / author's collection*

The geographic north pole, photographed from a DC-7C Seven Seas flown by SAS. *Courtesy of Gunnar Fahlgren*

Breakfast in bed on the way from Europe to Tokyo. *Courtesy of SAS Museum, Oslo*

Amundsen, the American millionaire Lincoln Ellsworth, and the Italian explorer Umberto Nobile took off from Spitsbergen in the airship Norge and reached Teller, Alaska, after the first crossing of the north polar ice desert by air. The navigator on the seventy-two-hour flight was the Norwegian general Hjalmar Riiser-Larsen, who would later play a leading role in planning the first SAS polar routes.

NAVIGATION OVER THE ARCTIC

The first considerations of regular air traffic across the North Pole began just one year after Scandinavian Airlines was founded. In the process, the Flying Vikings faced three fundamental challenges that no airline before them had been able to solve: the uselessness of magnetic compasses, the polar twilight, and the uselessness of conventional navigation charts when flying over the Arctic.

In those pioneering days of aviation, magnetic compasses were the standard instrument for course determination. They showed the crew the direction in which the aircraft was flying, and were thus an indispensable instrument then as now. However, when an aircraft approaches the North Pole, the compasses are so deflected by the strong magnetic fields that they spin wildly and are therefore useless for navigation. In addition, the magnetic north pole is not colocated with the geographic north pole and constantly changes its position. For reliable course determination, the magnetic compass thus fails completely.

Another problem the SAS Arctic pioneers faced was so-called Arctic twilight. At that time, long before the introduction of today's computer-based navigation instruments, navigators formed part of the crew on long-haul flights. Like ship's navigators, they used their sextants to determine the position of the aircraft either in relation to certain stars or the sun. In the periods around March 21 and September 21 each year, the sun is below the horizon line in the Arctic and thus cannot be used for navigation. But its rays are still so strong that it also blocks the light from the stars. Conventional sextants thus become unusable.

Rasmussen 1921 — 24
Amundsen wintered here, 1903 — 4 and 104 — 5
COPPERMINE
ANCHORAGE
The north magnetic pole was located here by the Englishman J. C. Ross in 1831.
Magnetic Pole
First explored by the Canadian Arctic Expedition of 1913 — 18 under Stefansson.
McClure 1850 — 54
Koch and Wegener 1913
These islands were first explored by the Norwegian Otto Sverdrup who spent four consecutive winters in the arctic, 1898 — 1902.
Paul-Emile Victor, 1948 — 51
Peary 1892
SAS pioneered regular routes over the Polar short cut by inaugurating scheduled services between Europe and California in November 1954, between Europe and Japan in February 1957.
The first air crossing of the Arctic Ocean was made in 1926, by Amundsen (Norway), Ellsworth (USA) and Nobile (Italy) in the airship "Norge".
Knud Rasmussen 1912
Dezhnev 1648 (USSR)
Peary 1909 (USA)
Peary, over ice, 1909
Byrd, by air, 1926
Anderson, by submarine, 1958
The Northeast Passage, from Europe to the Pacific, sought since the 16th century, was first achieved by the Swede Nordenskiöld in the "Vega" 1878 — 79.
Papanin 1937 — 38 (USSR)
"Nautilus" 1958
The Norwegian Nansen was the first to realise the importance of the Arctic ice-drift. In 1893 he set his ship "Fram" into the unnavigable Polar ice, with which it drifted for 3 years.
The Magnetic North Pole is the centre of the northern lights (aurora borealis). These colourful giant "light draperies" can usually be seen waving in the sky all the way between the coast of Norway and Anchorage, Alaska.
Although known to the Vikings, Spitsbergen was rediscovered by the Dutchman Barents in 1596.
Barents' expedition of 1596 wintered here, the first Europeans to do so in the arctic.
Named by the Swede Nordenskiöld for his Swedish patron, Oscar Dickson.
Frobisher 1576
FROBISHER BAY
Cumberland Sound
Davis Strait
GODTHAAB
HOLSTEINSBORG
OMFJORD
CHRISTIANSHAAB
GODHAVN
Disko Bugt
Disko
Parry 1819 — 20
Amundsen "Gjoa" 1903 — 07
UPERNAVIK
Baffin Bay
THULE
Hayes Peninsula
Smith Sound
Kane Basin
MOUNT FOREL 11,100
GREENLAND
GUNNBJØRNS FJÆLD 12,139
SCORESBYSUND
Scoresby Sund
Shannon Island
Nordost Rundingen
Denmarks Fjord
Independence Fjord
Peary Land
Victoria Fjord
Kap Morris Jesup
Kap Bridgman
Peary 1909
North Pole
GREENLAND SEA
Jan Mayen (Norway)
NORWEGIAN SEA
Arctic Circle is where the Midnight sun is clock in
Arctic circle
BODO
NARVIK
Lofoten
KIRUNA
LULEA
Nordkapp (North Cape)
MURMANSK
Novaya Zemlya
Matochkin Shar
Beloe More (White Sea)
Mys Kanin Nos
Ostrov Kolguyev
FINLAND
Poluostrov Kanin
Gulf of Bothnia
TURKU (ABO)
HELSINKI
KARA SEA
Ostrov Belyy
DIKSON
Ostrov Vaygach
Yamal Poluostrov
Gydanskiy Poluostrov
Obskaya Guba
Yenisej
Ob
NORTHWEST TERRITORIES
Foxe Peninsula
Foxe Basin
REPULSE BAY
King William Island
CAMBRIDGE BAY
READ ISLAND
Coronation Gulf
Amundsen Gulf
Cape Bathurst
Victoria Island
Boothia Peninsula
Prince Charles Island
Melville Peninsula
IGLOOLIK
CANADA
Baffin Island
PENNY HIGHLAND
Cape Dyer
PADLOPING ISLAND
Baffin Island
Somerset Island
ARCTIC BAY
Bylot Island
Devon Island
DUNDAS HARBOUR
Jones Sound
CRAIG HARBOUR
Ellesmere Island
Axel Heiberg Island
Lincoln Sea
ALERT
Victoria Fjord
Lancaster Sound
Cornwallis Island
Bathurst Island
RESOLUTE
Prince of Wales Island
FORT ROSS
Mc Clintock Channel
Prince of Wales Strait
HOLMAN ISLAND
Banks Island
Melville Island
Viscount Melville Sound
McClure Strait
QUEEN ELIZABETH ISLANDS
Sverdrup Islands
Mackenzie King Island
Prince Patrick Island
ISACHSEN
Borden Island
MOULD BAY
BEAUFORT SEA
Cape Halkett
Point Barrow
BARROW
Cape Lisburne
Point Hope
KOTZEBUE
Kotzebue Sound
NOME
Seward Peninsula
Norton Sound
BETHEL
Kuskokwim
Yukon River
FAIRBANKS
FORT YUKON
TANANA
ALASKA (USA)
Brooks Range
MT McKINLEY
MT MICHELSON
Martin Point
Mackenzie
STANTON
AKLAVIK
Alaska Range
NAKNEK
DILLINGHAM
Bering Strait
Diomede Islands (USA)
UELEN
PROVIDENIYA
CHUKCHI SEA
Chukotskiy Poluostrov
ANADYR
Anadyr Zal
UELLKAL
Ostrov Vrangelya (Wrangel Island)
PEVEK
Mys Shelagskiy
EAST SIBERIAN SEA
AMBARCHIK
NIZHNIYE KRESTY
Ostrov Novaya Sibir
Ostrov Faddeyevskiy
Ostrov Kotel'nyy
Novosibirskiye Ostrova (New Siberian Islands)
Ostrov Bol'shoy
ZYRYANKA
SREDNE-KOLYMSK
Indigirka
ARCTIC OCEAN
LAPTEV SEA
SOVIET UNION
Khrebet
VERKHOYANSK
Verkhoyanskiy Khrebet
Yana
Lena
TIKSI
Guba Buar-Khaya
KAZACH'YE
ZHIGANSK
SANGARE
SASKYLAKH
Ozero Taymyr
Poluostrov Taymyr
Severnaya Zemlya (North Land)
Ostrov Komsomolets
Ostrov Oktyabr'skoy Revolyutsii
Ostrov Bol'shevik
KHATANGA
NORDVIK
VOLOCHANKA
OLENEK
Zemlya Georga
Zemlya Aleksandry
Zemlya Frantsa Josifa (Franz Josef Land) (USSR)
Ostrov Graham Bell
Zemlya Vil'cheka
Ostrov Ushakova
Ostrov Graham Bell
SVALBARD (Norway)
LONGYEARBYEN
W. Spitsbergen
Edge øya
Bjørnøya (Bear Island)
Hopen
Northeast Land
Nordkapp
OLEKMINSK

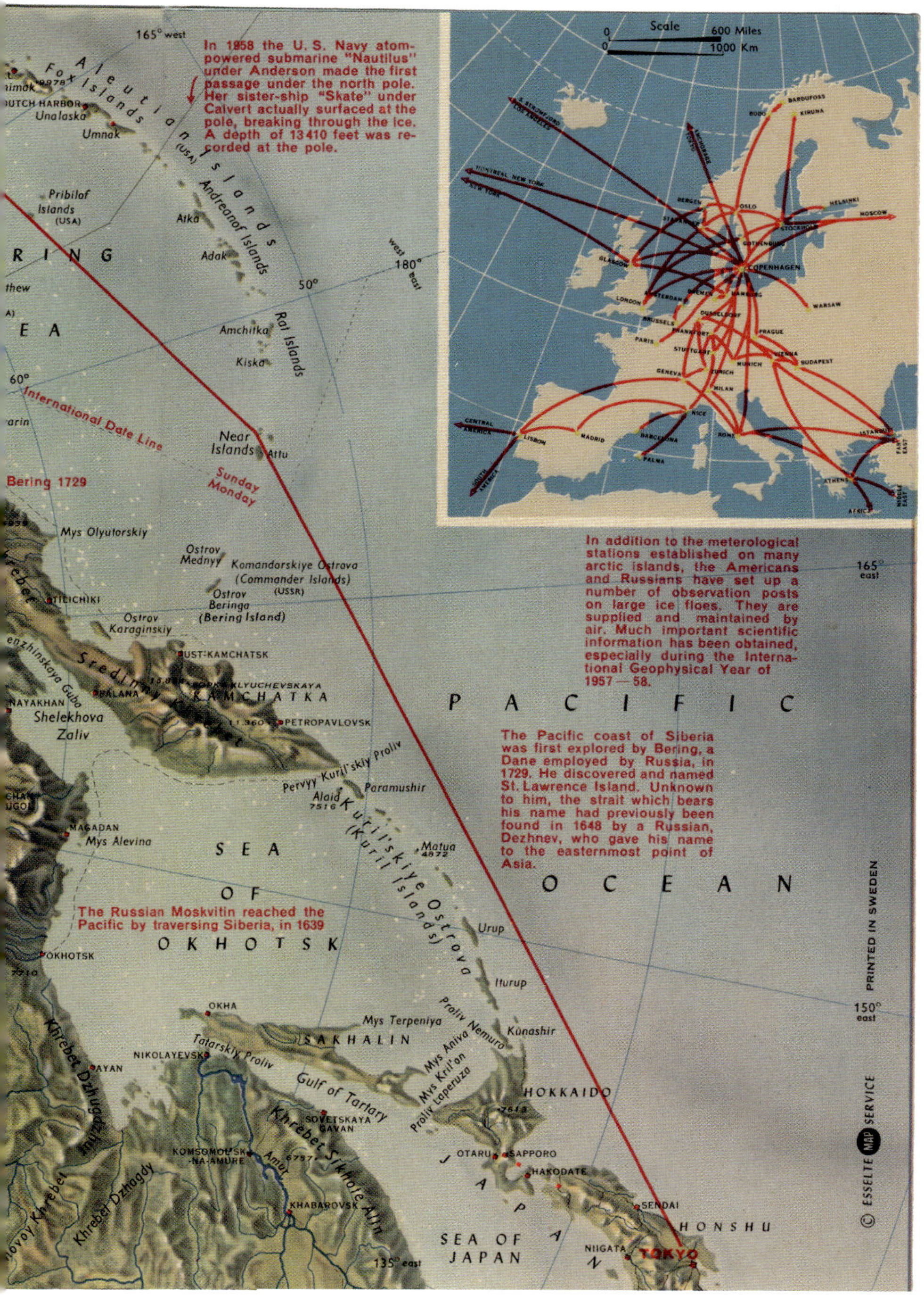
In 1958 the U. S. Navy atom-powered submarine "Nautilus" under Anderson made the first passage under the north pole. Her sister-ship "Skate" under Calvert actually surfaced at the pole, breaking through the ice. A depth of 13410 feet was recorded at the pole.
In addition to the meterological stations established on many arctic islands, the Americans and Russians have set up a number of observation posts on large ice floes. They are supplied and maintained by air. Much important scientific information has been obtained, especially during the International Geophysical Year of 1957 — 58.
The Pacific coast of Siberia was first explored by Bering, a Dane employed by Russia, in 1729. He discovered and named St. Lawrence Island. Unknown to him, the strait which bears his name had previously been found in 1648 by a Russian, Dezhnev, who gave his name to the easternmost point of Asia.
The Russian Moskvitin reached the Pacific by traversing Siberia, in 1639
Bering 1729
International Date Line
Sunday
Monday
PACIFIC OCEAN
SEA OF OKHOTSK
SEA OF JAPAN
KAMCHATKA
SAKHALIN
HOKKAIDO
HONSHU
TOKYO
Scale
600 Miles
1000 Km
COPENHAGEN
PRINTED IN SWEDEN
© ESSELTE MAP SERVICE

DIE
Einzigartige
DC7C
SAS
GLOBAL EXPRESS

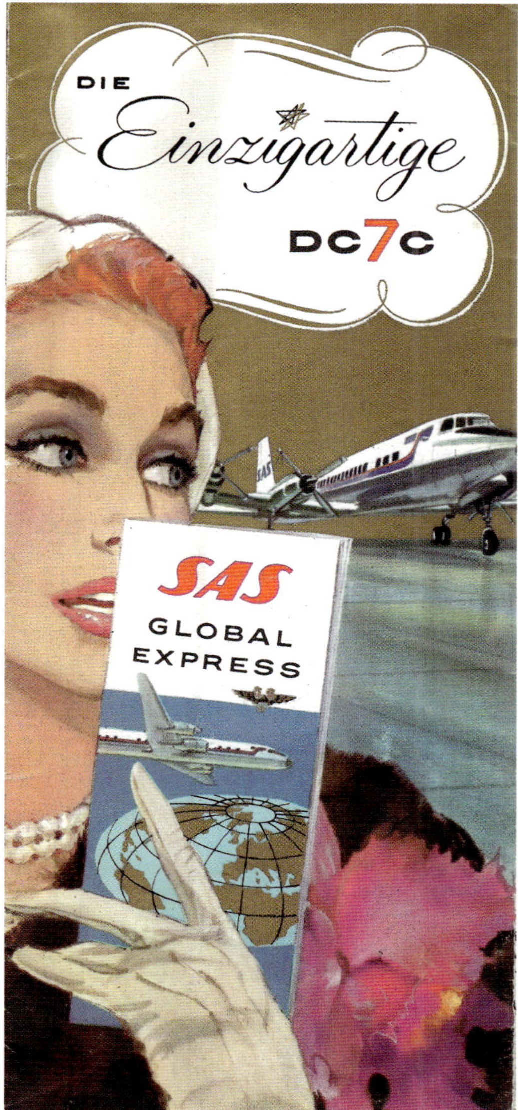

This map published by SAS in the 1950s shows the flight route taken by its aircraft over the North Pole. The Norwegian port of Bodö is shown at the bottom left; Anchorage, Alaska, is at the top center; and the Japanese capital, Tokyo, is at the bottom right as the destination of the polar route. *Courtesy of SAS / author's collection*

"The Unique DC-7C," SAS leaflet advertising a flight on their "Seven Seas." *Courtesy of SAS / author's collection*

SAS published boarding postcards of their DC-6B and DC-7C (*photo*) with this polar motif of a Douglas airliner flying over an Inuit boy. *Courtesy of SAS / author's collection*

The band of Copenhagen's world-famous Tivoli amusement park played on the occasion of the farewell of the first SAS scheduled flight from Copenhagen, via Anchorage to Tokyo. *Courtesy of SAS Museum, Oslo*

SAS chief navigator Einar Sverre Pedersen determining a course over the Arctic with the help of the Kollsman Sky Compass. *Courtesy of SAS / author's collection*

The SAS premier flight over the North Pole was received as ceremoniously in Tokyo as it was seen off in Copenhagen. *Courtesy of SAS Museum, Oslo*

The famous four-person Arctic survival bag is on display at the Polar exhibit of the SAS Museum in Oslo, Norway. *Author's collection*

Conventional navigation maps cannot be used, because the meridians converge at the geographic pole. There is simply no longer any indication of direction in the classical sense. If you are "on top of the world," any direction is south.

As a solution to these three fundamental navigation problems, SAS, in cooperation with the leading companies in the aerospace industry at the time, developed various technical solutions that enabled safe flight operations over the polar region. In addition to its own developments and those of its industrial partners, the airline used knowledge gained from the American and Canadian air forces during the Second World War. However, it took not just one or two, but three systems tailor-made for SAS to achieve success. These were the so-called Bendix "Polar Path Gyro," the Kollsman "Sky Compass," and the SAS "Polar Grid Chart." The Polar Path Gyro worked like a pathfinder, keeping the aircraft on the course chosen by the crew. The core of the spherical device, the size of an orange, was a gyro that stabilized itself at 23,000 revolutions per minute. Like a humming top for children, the electrically driven instrument maintained its position in space—and reliably kept the machine's autopilot on course. The Kollsman Sky Compass, mounted on the periscope, also solved the problem of polar twilight. It made the rays emitted by the setting sun and hitting the atmosphere visible again in so-called polarized bands. These bands pointed in the direction of the sun, so that it could be used as a navigation point at any time. Finally, SAS navigators used the Polar Grid Chart to determine their position. Their grid replaced the conventional division into lines of longitude and latitude, which an aircraft passed at ever-shorter intervals as it approached the North Pole, until there was only one course to the south. The grid map, with the North Pole at its center, replaced the division of the polar region by parallel vertical and horizontal lines, familiar from atlases and globes. Since there were no reliable navigation charts for civil aviation over the North Pole toward the end of the 1940s, SAS had to obtain very detailed charts for the company's own grid charts from US military and Russian sources. In addition, SAS invested large sums in setting up radio stations in the perpetual ice, which received position reports from the aircraft and forwarded them to its own operations center in Scandinavia.

After the lengthy preliminary work was done, an SAS Douglas DC-6B took off from Los Angeles, California, on November 19, 1952, for the first Arctic flight by a commercial aircraft from the American West Coast, via Edmonton (Canada) and Thule (Greenland) to the Danish capital of Copenhagen. Further tests followed on later delivery flights of brand-new Douglas DC-6Bs to Denmark. One of these was the first flight with passengers and mail on December 5–6, 1952. In 1954, the SAS pioneers finally felt ready to launch the first scheduled commercial service over the Arctic. On November 15 of that year, the DC-6B "Helge Viking" took off in a flurry of flashbulbs from the world press for the flight from Copenhagen to Los Angeles. For several years, SAS remained unrivaled with this fastest connection between California and Europe!

But the Scandinavians were not yet satisfied with this success.

Because another challenge awaited much farther north. After the direct flight path on the great circle between Europe and Japan, across the territory of the USSR, was barred to Western airlines during the Cold War, the North Pole route via Alaska was considered the shortest and thus fastest possible flight connection to the Far East. The airline that was the first to offer this route was therefore guaranteed stable ticket and freight revenues for many years. Motivated by this, SAS set out to explore this uncharted territory, into which no other airline had ventured before.

After a series of test flights with only the crews on board, the first flight with passengers and cargo over the geographic North Pole took place in May 1954. The DC-6B flew nonstop from Bodø in northern Norway to Fairbanks, Alaska, and from there to Tokyo via Shemya in the Aleutian Islands. On the way back from Tokyo, via Fairbanks to Stockholm, it was fully loaded with cargo. In April 1956, the Vienna Philharmonic orchestra chartered an SAS DC-6B for a concert tour from Austria to Japan. The entire ensemble, including instruments, also took the shortcut over the Pole.

The SAS Polar Cocktail was part of the standard transpolar drinks bar on board the DC-7C (*photo*). *Courtesy of SAS Museum, Oslo*

The luxury in the Golden Age of Air Transport. *Courtesy of SAS Museum, Oslo*

In the summer of 1956, SAS took delivery of the first of fourteen Douglas DC-7C Seven Seas, with greater passenger capacity, speed, and range compared to the DC-6B. In October 1956, one of the delivery flights was diverted from Santa Monica, California, via Anchorage and the North Pole to Scandinavia to test the plane's polar capability. The results were so promising that SAS scheduled five DC-7Cs carrying the Olympic teams of nine European nations over the North Pole to the Summer Olympics in Melbourne, Australia, that same month. Five more months were to pass before the first scheduled flight of an SAS DC-7C over the North Pole. Finally, with a big celebration in Copenhagen, "Guttorm Viking" took off on February 24, 1957, for the flight via Anchorage to Tokyo. The route explored by SAS nearly halved the travel time between northern Europe and Japan from fifty-two to twenty-seven hours. The DC-7C that carried out the first flight returned to Denmark four days later with another record. It was the first passenger aircraft to circumnavigate the globe on a commercial flight, in a record time of seventy-one hours and six minutes. These pioneering achievements were henceforth emblazoned on the passenger doors of the SAS long-haul fleet: "First over the Pole—and around the World." In 1962, SAS became the first airline in the world to be awarded the prestigious Christopher Columbus Prize by the city of Genoa in recognition of its exploration of polar aviation.

THE POLAR COCKTAIL

When the Douglas DC-7C "Guttorm Viking" took to the skies at Copenhagen on February 24, 1954, bound for Anchorage and Tokyo, not only did it have an illustrious crowd of guests on board for this premier flight over the North Pole. The onboard bar was equally well stocked, helping the invited guests to make the long flight time seem a lot more entertaining. The Brussels bartender Léopold Douchar created the SAS Polar Cocktail especially for this flight on behalf of the airline. According to tradition, it consisted of the following ingredients:

¼ Cherry Heering (a Danish cherry-flavored liqueur)

¼ Cointreau

¼ Rhum Negrita (a Caribbean rum)

¼ Noilly Prat French Vermouth

The whole decorated with a sour cherry.

While the guests of honor were enjoying themselves not only with this drink in the passenger cabin, farther ahead the cockpit crew was navigating the Douglas DC-7C across the Arctic Ocean with zero alcohol in their blood. To enable accurate timekeeping even in these extreme regions, SAS had commissioned the Swiss watch manufacturer Universal Genève to develop and produce special wristwatches that would be resistant to the strong magnetic fields in the polar region. In the 1950s and 1960s, every SAS pilot, flight engineer, and navigator on the North Pole route to Los Angeles, Anchorage, and Tokyo wore one of these "Polarouter" watches with the SAS logo on the dial. Universal Genève used the worldwide media response to the opening of the first scheduled connections across the Arctic Ocean for the commercial sale of this watch developed for SAS. Now called the "Polerouter" for public sale, Universal Genève, in collaboration with SAS, even advertised its elegant chronometers in flight schedules in the 1950s.

CHAPTER 9
DC-4E, DC-4, DC-6, AND DC-7 SPECIFICATIONS

This DC-7C, registration VR-BCW, of ARCO Bermuda paid a visit to Copenhagen airport on August 31, 1969. *Courtesy of Tom Weihe*

DOUGLAS FOUR-ENGINE PROPLINER SPECIFICATIONS

DC-4 EXPERIMENTAL	
Dimensions	
Span (ft.)	138 ft., 3 in.
Fuselage length (ft.)	97 ft., 7 in.
Maximum height (ft.)	24 ft., 6.5 in.
Max. Wing Thickness	54 in.
Engines	4 x Pratt & Whitney R-2180-S1A1-G Twin Hornet
Propeller diameter in ft.	14
Max. hp for take-off (all four engines)	5,600
Weights	
Gross weight (lbs.)	65,000
Useful load (lbs.)	20,000
Performance	
High speed (mph)	240
Cruising speed at 65% power (mph)	200
Corresponding altitude (ft.)	10,000
Landing speed (mph)	69
Service ceiling (ft.)	22,900
Absolute ceiling (ft.)	24,000
Maximum fuel (gals.)	2,050
Maximum cruising range (mi.)	2,200
Accommodations	
Max. Passengers	42
Luxury daytime accommodation	40
Luxury night-time accommodation in berths	32
Items of interest	
Engineering time (hrs.)	500,000
Laboratory testing time (hrs.)	100,000
Number of drawings and blueprints	8,100
Rivets used	1,300,000
Source	Douglas Aircraft Company DC-4E brochure 1939

DATA SHEET DOUGLAS FOUR-ENGINED PROPLINERS

DC-4	
Dimensions	
Span (ft.)	117 ft., 6 in.
Fuselage length (ft.)	93 ft., 5 in.
Maximum height (ft.)	27 ft., 7 in.
Wing area	1,460 sq. ft.
Engines	4 x Pratt & Whitney R-2000 Twin Wasp
Propeller diameter in ft.	13 ft., 1 in.
Max. hp for take-off (all four engines)	5,800
Weights	
Gross weight (lbs.)	63,500
Useful load (lbs.)	26,000
Performance	
Max. speed (mph)	280
Cruising speed at 60% power (mph)	227
Operating altitude (ft.)	10,000
Service ceiling (ft.)	22,900
Absolute ceiling (ft.)	24,000
Maximum fuel (gals.)	3,600
Maximum cruising range (mi.)	4,255
Accommodations	
Max. Passengers	86
Luxury daytime accommodation	44
Luxury nighttime accommodation in berths	22
Items of interest	
Laboratory testing time (hrs.)	100,000
Number of drawings and blueprints	8,100
Rivets used	1,300,000
Source	Douglas Aircraft Company

	Douglas DC-6	DC-6A Freighter	DC-6B	DC-7C
Dimensions				
Span (ft.)	117 ft., 6 in.	117 ft., 6 in.	117 ft., 6 in.	127 ft., 6 in.
Length (ft.)	100 ft., 7 in.	105 ft., 7 in.	105 ft., 7 in.	112 ft., 3 in.
Height (ft.)	28 ft., 5 in.	28 ft., 5 in.	28 ft., 5 in.	31 ft., 8 in.
Wing area (sq. ft.)	1,463	1,463	1,463	1,637
Engines	4 x Pratt & Whitney R-2800	4 x Pratt & Whitney R-2800	4 x Pratt & Whitney R-2800	4 x Wright R-3350-988TC18EA1-2
Max. hp for take-off (all four engines)	9,600	9,600	10,000	13,600
Weights				
Empty weight (lbs.)	52,567	45,862	55,357	72,763
Max. gross take-off weight (lbs.)	97,200	107,200	107,000	143,000
Performan				
Cruising speed (mph)	311	315	315	346
Max. range at full payload (nm.)	3,983	2,948 (max. payload)	2,610 (max. payload)	4,028 (max. payload)
Service ceiling (ft.)	21,900	21,900	25,000	21,700
Accommodations				
Max. passengers	68	0	89	105
Max. cargo capacity as all freighter (lbs.)		28,188		

Canadair C-4 North Star	
Dimensions	
Span (ft.)	117 ft., 6 in.
Length (ft.)	93 ft., 7.5 in.
Height (ft.)	27 ft., 6 in.
Wing area (sq. ft.)	1,457
Engines	4 x Rolls-Royce Merlin 624 or 724
Max. hp for take-off (all four engines)	7,040
Weights	
Operating weight empty (lbs.)	49,230
Max. gross take-off weight (lbs.)	82,000
Max. landing weight (lbs.)	72,000
Max. zero fuel weight (lbs.)	68,000
Performance	
Cruising speed (mph)	280
Corresponding altitude (ft.)	20,000
Max. range at full payload (mi.)	3,100
Accommodations	
Max. passengers on charter operations with Derby Airways	78
North Star Freigher max. payload (lbs.)	18,970

ATL-98 Carvair	
Dimensions	
Span (ft.)	117 ft., 6 in.
Length (ft.)	102 ft., 7 in.
Height (ft.)	29 ft., 10 in.
Wing area (sq. ft.)	1,462
Engines	Pratt & Whitney R-2000-7M2
Propeller diameter in ft.	13 ft., 1 in.
Max. h.p. for take-off (all four engines)	5,800
Weights	
Empty weight (lbs.)	41,365
Max. take-off weight (lbs.)	73,800
Performance	
Max. speed (mph)	250
Cruising speed (mph)	213
Max. range at max. payload (mi.)	2,300
Corresponding altitude in ft.	10,000
Service ceiling (ft.)	18,700
Accommodations	
Max. load (passengers + small sized cars)	23 + 6
Rear passenger cabin length	13 ft., 2 in.
Main cargo compartment length as full freighter	80 ft., 1 in.

Not in one of America's famous aviation museums, but on the edge of a parking lot in the Lower Saxon municipality of Bad Laer, Germany, a special treasure of civil aviation history can be found. Here, in the immediate vicinity of a health and shopping center, the oldest Douglas DC-6 still in existence today braves wind and bad weather. The fourth "Cloudmaster" built by Douglas in Santa Monica, California, took off on its maiden flight on November 24, 1946, and was handed over to the DC-6's launch customer, American Airlines, in March 1947. *Author's collection*

Internord Aviation A/S was a Danish charter airline founded as a joint venture between Ostermann Air Charter of Sweden and Aero-Nord of Denmark. In addition to DC-7s and DC-7Cs, Internord also flew four-engined Convair 990 jet airliners, which it purchased secondhand. Since these aircraft, which were very expensive to maintain and operate, could not be used to capacity, the airline had to file for bankruptcy again in 1968. *Courtesy of Tom Weihe*

Südflug was based at Stuttgart airport in southern Germany. The company, founded by former German fighter pilot Rul Bückle in 1952, was acquired by Lufthansa in 1968 and integrated into its then subsidiary Condor Flugdienst. D-ABAS, which was photographed at Copenhagen on May 29, 1966, was one of six Südflug DC-7Cs. *Courtesy of Tom Weihe*

The story of the DC-7B in this photograph, which was leased by the Swedish airline Transair to Turkish Airlines, was overshadowed by an accident on January 20, 1968, while landing at Munich-Riem. The cause was a collapsed nose gear during touchdown. When photographed at Copenhagen on September 17, 1967, SE-ERC was still in top technical condition. *Courtesy of Tom Weihe*

Like Sterling, Conair of Scandinavia was a longtime Danish charter airline, which from 1965 onward flew mainly for Spies Rejser, another Danish tour operator. In 1994, Conair merged with the SAS charter subsidiary Scanair to form Premiair. After further renaming, it lived on in the airline Sunclass in autumn 2022. This photo of Conair's DC-7 OY-DMU was taken on June 12, 1967. *Courtesy of Tom Weihe*

CHAPTER 10
COMPETING PROPELLER-DRIVEN AIRLINERS OF THE DOUGLAS FOUR-ENGINED PROPLINER ERA

South Africa's Johannesburg Airport was one of the far-flung destinations of the BOAC Avro York fleet. *Courtesy of Transnet*

AVRO 685 YORK

Manufacturer	A. V. Roe & Company Ltd., Great Britain
First flight	July 5, 1942
Number built	253
Wingspan	102 ft.
Length	78 ft.
Height	17 ft.
Power plants	4 × Rolls-Royce Merlin 502
Cruise	approx. 220 mph
Range	approx. 1,079 nautical miles

CIVIL LANCASTER CONVERSION KITS

Like the Avro Tudor, the York was a further development of the Lancaster bomber design, from which it "inherited" the wings, landing gear, Rolls-Royce Merlin engines, and tail unit. These assemblies were supplemented by a new, box-shaped fuselage on which a third vertical stabilizer provided better maneuverability. First introduced into service by the Royal Air Force as a troop carrier and freighter in 1942, the York found new civilian use after the end of the war with British Overseas Airways Corporation (BOAC) and British South American Airways (BSAA), as well as Argentina's Flota Aérea Mercante Argentina (FAMA). BOAC used its Yorks mainly on routes to West Africa and South Africa, as far as Johannesburg. BSAA Yorks, on the other hand, flew from London to destinations in the Caribbean, as well as on the South American continent. Often the flight altitude over the ocean was only a few hundred feet. This was especially true for flights in a westerly direction, to avoid the prevailing strong headwinds at higher altitudes. Flying under bad weather was often the only alternative, since the York did not have a pressurized cabin for higher altitudes. In addition to the state airlines BOAC and BSAA, which merged in 1949, almost every private British charter airline in the postwar period also flew the reliable York. The largest fleets were operated by Dan-Air London and Skyways, which carried charter passengers to holiday destinations and, above all, British troops to theaters of operations around the globe. Three British airlines—Airflight, Skyways, and BSAA, as well as the Royal Air Force, were involved in the Berlin Airlift of 1948–49 with a total of thirty-five Yorks. This type of aircraft was the backbone of British participation in supplying West Berlin by air, carrying 61 percent of the cargo flown and a 42 percent share of British movements through the two air corridors used by Britain. The last two of 253 Avro 685s built are on display at the British Air Force Museum in Cosford and the Imperial War Museum in Duxford.

The first-class service offered by the airlines on board the Stratocruiser was hard to beat in terms of luxury and an homage to the glorious Boeing 314 Clipper flying boats from the days before the beginning of the Second World War. *Courtesy of Boeing*

THE BOEING 377 STRATOCRUISER

Manufacturer	Boeing Aircraft Company, Seattle
First flight	July 8, 1947
Number built	56
Wingspan	141 ft.
Length	110 ft.
Height	38 ft.
Power plants	4 × Pratt & Whitney R-4360
Cruise	approx. 340 mph
Range	approx. 3,509 nautical miles

LUXURY ABOVE THE CLOUDS

With the Boeing Stratocruiser, in the late 1940s launch customer Pan American Airways (PAA) emulated the glamour and luxury offered on board the airline's legendary Clipper flying boats in the prewar years. On its two passenger decks, connected by a spiral staircase, the Boeing 377 offered everything the discerning traveling public of the time expected. This included men's and women's dressing rooms and washrooms as well as toilets. There was an en extensive galley where the seven-course menus of the President First Class Service were prepared, as well as a cocktail bar in the lower deck where the illustrious company gathered for a drink after the opulent meal. Horizontally folding reclining seats and real beds with mattresses, pillows, and duvets ensured a relaxed sleep even on long night flights. Two- and four-bed cabins could also be hired on board the PAA Stratocruiser for very private luxury. Five stewardesses and stewards looked after a maximum of forty-seven passengers.

An evolution of the Model 367, the Boeing 377 shared the final-assembly line in Seattle with the manufacturer's B-50 long-range bombers. The similarities between the two models involved several structural elements and systems, including the vertical tail and the Pratt & Whitney R-4360 Wasp Major engines. On top of the B-50's lower fuselage shell, Boeing placed the upper, wider passenger cabin, making the Stratocruiser fuselage look like an upside-down figure eight when viewed from the front.

Boeing produced a total of 888 Model 367s from 1944 to June 1956, which were used as C-97 transports under the name Stratofreighter and as KC-97 Stratotankers for air-to-air refueling of military aircraft. The Boeing 377 looks very similar to its military sister on the outside but differs from the Boeing 367 in various ways. Boeing invested about four million engineering hours in further developing it into a reliable and comfortable commercial aircraft. The prototype took off on its first flight on July 8, 1947—a year later than originally planned. And another year and a half would pass before Pan American could take delivery of its first Boeing 377 on January 31, 1949. During the test phase, the Pratt & Whitney Wasp Major engines, which were prone to failure, were a particular cause for concern. A problem that could never be completely solved by the engine manufacturer led to various accidents and fatal crashes during the Stratocruiser's service life. A total of fifty-six Boeing 377 Stratocruisers

were produced, and the type was initially flown by Pan American, American Overseas Airlines, and BOAC.

HANDLEY PAGE H.P. 81 HERMES

Manufacturer	Handley Page, Radlett, Great Britain
First flight	December 2, 1945 (Hermes I)
Number built	27 (1 Hermes I, 1 Hermes II, 25 Hermes IV)
Wingspan	113 ft.
Length	97 ft.
Height	30 ft.
Power plants	4 × Bristol Hercules 763
Cruise	approx. 270 mph
Range	approx. 1,619 nautical miles
Crew	4 on the flight deck (long-range flights) plus 2 in the cabin

The Handley Page Hermes was designed as the first British postwar long-range type for the BOAC. However, its performance was disappointing, lagging far behind that of the American and Canadian competition. BOAC was forced to order Lockheed Constellations and Canadair Argonauts as economic alternatives. *Author's archive*

TAILOR-MADE, BUT UNPOPULAR

The Handley Page Hermes IV was the first large British-built airliner to go into series production after the end of the Second World War. Only twenty-five examples were built at Radlett (near London), exclusively for the British Overseas Airways Corporation (BOAC). Although this model was tailor-made for BOAC and its route network, the airline was particularly disappointed with the economic efficiency of its Hermes IV and withdrew the entire fleet after only four years of service. The Hermes project was ill fated from the start, after the prototype Hermes I, with the registration G-AGSS, went out of control shortly after takeoff on its maiden flight on December 2, 1945, and crashed. Handley Page's chief test pilot Jimmy Talbot and engineer "Ginger" Wright, who was flying as an observer in the right seat, lost their lives. The cause of the accident was quickly determined to be an incorrectly mounted trim tab that made it impossible to control the aircraft. Although no fundamental error in the aircraft design was responsible for the accident, Handley Page initially postponed the development of the civilian Hermes in favor of its military sister, the Hastings.

When the Handley Page team returned to the Hermes, the engineers replaced the original tailwheel undercarriage with a more modern design of a transport aircraft with a more current tricycle undercarriage. The Hermes IV of 1948 was very advanced for its time, featuring not only an extremely comfortable pressurized cabin, but also air-conditioning with humidity control. An innovation at the time, which Boeing boasted only a few years ago was a novelty on its 787 Dreamliner.

The Hermes IV was first used on BOAC's routes to the former British colonies on the African continent. In addition to its poor profitability, the entry into service of the world's first jet airliner, the de Havilland Comet 1, in 1952 led to the gradual replacement of the Hermes IV fleet at BOAC. It was not until the series of accidents involving the Comet 1 and its subsequent grounding that the Hermes IV fleet, which had already been decommissioned, made a brief comeback from the summer of 1954. The Hermes were used mainly on the Nairobi route until December 2 of that year. The aircraft taken out of service by BOAC met with brisk demand from British charter airlines. The last Hermes IV was not taken out of service by Air Links until 1964. Unfortunately, no complete example of this type has survived. Only the fully equipped fuselage of the Hermes IV, once registered G-ALDG, has been restored and can be admired in BOAC colors at the British Aviation Museum in Duxford.

LOCKHEED L-049 CONSTELLATION

Manufacturer	Lockheed Aircraft Corp., Burbank, CA
First flight	January 9, 1943 (C-69 prototype)
Number built	88 (C-69 and L-049)
Wingspan	123 ft.
Length	95 ft.
Height	23 ft.
Power plants	4 × Wright Duplex Cyclone R-3350
Cruise	approx. 270 mph
Range	approx. 1,898 nautical miles
Crew	3–5 on the flight deck (long-range flights) plus 3 in the cabin

Development of the Lockheed Constellation was a secret project involving the charismatic and eccentric entrepreneur Howard Hughes, TWA, which he controlled, and the Lockheed company management. However, the planned, initially exclusive entry into service of the first L-049 in service with Transcontinental & Western Air (TWA) was preempted by the American entry into the Second World War. *Courtesy of Lockheed Martin*

THE BIRTH OF A LEGEND

After Pan American Airways (PAA) had rejected Lockheed's proposed Excalibur design for a fast commercial aircraft in 1937, Howard Hughes's hour had come. The eccentric, aviation-mad multibillionaire recognized the opportunity he had with the unique Lockheed team of Bob Gross, Hall Hibbard, and chief designer Kelly Johnson. The young entrepreneurs had acquired the ailing Lockheed company only a few years earlier and were now in the process of rebuilding the company and realizing their dreams. What Hughes asked for was very much to the taste of the Lockheed team: a design that combined speed, range, and passenger comfort. From the very outset, Kelly Johnson's design signature made it clear that the Constellation would be an extraordinary aircraft. The curved dolphin-shaped fuselage, the triple tail unit, the enlarged wings of the Lockheed P-38 Lightning, and a speed of 340 miles per hour excited not only Hughes but also TWA president Jack Frye. He had persuaded Hughes to join the airline, which was now on its way to making history with the Constellation. The design presented by Gross, Hibbard, and Johnson was not only elegant, but above all captivating in its aerodynamic perfection. The dolphin-like all-metal fuselage formed an aerodynamically optimal unit with the wings. Four eighteen-cylinder Wright Duplex Cyclone R-3350 radial engines also developed a then-remarkable takeoff power of 2,200 hp each.

Howard Hughes feared nothing more than that the competition, especially Pan American Airways (PAA) president and archrival Juan Trippe, would find out about his plans. After long secret negotiations, Hughes was able to secure a contractual agreement that the first forty Constellation aircraft would be built exclusively for TWA at a unit price of 425,000 US dollars. Lockheed was not even permitted to hold sales talks with other airlines until after delivery of the thirty-fifth copy to Hughes. Production of the Model 049 Constellation began in 1940 with the forty examples for the Hughes Tool Company. Pan American Airways followed on June 11, 1940, with an order for forty aircraft. Howard Hughes agreed to this order only on the condition that PAA could use its "Connies" only on international routes. But neither the domestically strong TWA nor PAA as an intercontinental airline was to receive their aircraft as planned. On December 7, 1941, the Japanese navy attacked the US naval base at Pearl Harbor in Hawaii. Caught completely by surprise by the attack, the United States declared war on Japan one day later and was thus drawn into the turmoil of the Second World War from its once-neutral position. All production of civilian aircraft had to be halted immediately in favor of war equipment.

On January 9, 1943, the Constellation prototype in the form of the C-69 military version took off from the Lockheed Air Terminal in Burbank, California, on its maiden flight. Test pilot Edmund T. Allen was so pleased with the flight characteristics of the new aircraft that he carried out six test flights on the first day. Flight testing progressed well until a design flaw in the installed Wright R-3350 engines forced a temporary grounding on February 20, 1943, which was not removed until improved R-3350s were delivered in June of that year.

It was in keeping with the idiosyncratic character of Howard Hughes that he ignored official instructions and set off on a record-breaking flight from the Lockheed Air Terminal to Washington, DC, in the second C-69 prototype intended for the US Air Force but wearing full TWA colors. Hughes and Jack Frye covered the distance nonstop in a record time of six hours and fifty-eight minutes on April 17, 1944. Their average airspeed was 331 miles per hour. Hughes thus broke his transcontinental speed record, set seven years earlier, by just 3.3 miles per hour. He wanted the world to see what the "Connie" he had initiated was capable of!

By spring 1945, the US Army Air Force had ordered seventy-three C-69s, twenty-three of which were handed over to the military by the time of the armistice. The remaining fifty "Connies" ordered were promptly canceled after the guns fell silent. Lockheed president Bob Gross had these machines, most of which were already under construction, converted into passenger aircraft with minimal effort. They received their US civil certification as the Lockheed L-049 on December 11, 1945.

The first L-049 Constellations were delivered to the launch customers from prewar days, TWA and Pan Am, at the end of 1945. Other early customers included American Overseas Airlines, Air France, BOAC, KLM, and Panair do Brasil. From the L-049, development of the type led to the L-649—and finally the L-749A. It was the final, civil version of the original Constellation series and featured more-powerful engines, greater range, and a higher takeoff weight compared to its equally elegant predecessors.

LOCKHEED L-1049

SUPER CONSTELLATION

Manufacturer	Lockheed Aircraft Corp., Burbank, CA
First flight	October 13, 1950 (lengthened C-69 prototype)
Number built	104 (L-1049G version)
Wingspan	123 ft.
Length	114 ft.
Height	25 ft.
Power plants	4 × Wright Turbo-Compound 972 TC 18 DA-3
Cruise	approx. 330 mph
Range	approx. 4,813 nautical miles (0 wind, 0 payload)
Crew	6 on the flight deck (long-range flights) plus 4 in the cabin

THE QUEEN OF THE NORTH ATLANTIC

Following the L-749, the next generation of the Constellation series was launched on October 13, 1950, in the form of the Lockheed L-1049 Super Constellation. The aircraft was an old acquaintance, since Lockheed had simply stretched the fuselage of the C-69 prototype with the construction number 1961 by 18.4 feet to create the prototype of the Super Connie. Before that, however, the manufacturer had

to buy back the original prototype, which had initially been sold to Howard Hughes, for 100,000 US dollars. To save time, the Pratt & Whitney R-2800 engines that had been installed in the meantime remained on the aircraft when flight trials began. Only after twenty-two hours of flight did the Lockheed test team replace 1961's power plants with the more powerful Wright Cyclone R-3350 C18 CA1 series engines. At 2,700 hp, the output of these twin-row piston engines was still far below that of the 3,400 hp R-3350 "turbo compound" versions. Their three "power recovery turbines" (PRT) per engine were coupled to the engine's crankshaft via different reduction gears. They were driven by the hot, very high-speed exhaust gases and thus contributed directly to the power increase of the engine. Since the US military initially claimed the new turbocompound technology for itself, it was not available for the civil Super Constellation until 1953. Thus, the 3,250 hp Wright Cyclone R-3350-972-TC18DA-1 turbocompound engines were first used in an L-1049C of the Dutch airline KLM, followed by the L-1049D cargo version, which Seaboard & Western placed into service as the first customer from 1954.

To save costs, Lockheed bought back the prototype of the Constellation with the construction number 1961 for 100,000 US dollars from Howard Hughes and, without further ado, stretched it into the prototype of the Super Constellation. This L-1049 made its first flight on October 13, 1950. *Courtesy of Lockheed Martin*

By far the most successful model of the Super Constellation series, however, was the L-1049G—called the Super G by Lufthansa at the time. With its distinctive wingtip fuel tanks, its elegant appearance contributed much to the Lockheed Super Constellation myth. The "Super G," on the other hand, owed its dubious reputation as the "most beautiful three-engined aircraft in the world" to the unreliability of its four Curtiss Wright R-3350 engines. The L-1049G was certified for flight on January 14, 1955, and the 104 examples of this bestselling Super Constellation that were completed were among the flagships of long-haul flights for airlines around the globe for many years. In June 1955, Lockheed announced the development of another variant, called the L-1049H. This combination version could be used both as a freighter and for passenger service. Flying Tiger Line was the first customer for this last civil version of the L-1049, which was equipped with further improved R-3350-972-TC18EA-3 "turbo compound" engines, each producing 3,400 hp for takeoff.

LOCKHEED L-1649A STARLINER

Manufacturer	Lockheed Aircraft Corp., Burbank, CA
First flight	October 10, 1956
Number built	44
Wingspan	150 ft.
Length	116 ft.
Height	24 ft.
Power plants	4 × Wright Turbo Compound 988 TC 18 EA-2
Cruise	approx. 340 mph
Range	approx. 6,101 nautical miles (0 wind, 0 payload)
Crew	6 on the flight deck (long-range flights) plus 4 in the cabin

THE LOCKHEED GRAND FINALE

The Lockheed L-1649A was an unloved child. The fleet planners of the launch customer TWA rejected it as uneconomical, since the jet age, with much-faster aircraft types, was just around the corner. Even Lockheed tried to prevent production at the last second by canceling the sales contract with TWA, since they saw no sales opportunities—only aviation tycoon Howard Hughes, owner of TWA at the time, persistently held on to his order for the final version of the legendary Constellation series, against the advice of his closest confidants. Development of the L-1649A with Curtiss Wright piston engines initially began as a turboprop with the type designation L-1449. It was supposed to make TWA competitive again in the competition with

Neither the management of the launch customer TWA nor Lockheed wanted to build the L-1649A Starliner. But Howard Hughes insisted on fulfilling a contract that forced his own airline to take delivery of those twenty-five L-1649As that Lockheed reluctantly had to build for him. The last and certainly most elegant version of the Constellation series came onto the market at the dawn of the jet age, when the era of piston engines on long-haul routes was finally a thing of the past. It was therefore not surprising that, apart from TWA, which had been conscripted by its owner, only two other customers were found—Air France and Lufthansa, and that only forty-four examples were built in Burbank, California. *Courtesy of Lufthansa*

the Douglas DC-7C of other airlines. The Douglas Seven Seas, announced in 1954, overtook TWA's Lockheed L-1049G, and not just in terms of cruising speed. Its long range also made refueling stops on the route between the US and Europe and on the connections between the American East and West Coasts unnecessary. Fearing competitive disadvantages, TWA management initially considered ordering DC-7Cs themselves when rumors circulated that Lockheed was working on a "long thin wing" for a turboprop version of the Constellation, which would allow not only higher cruising speeds but also a comparable range to the DC-7C—the L-1449 project was born. In the autumn of 1954, Howard Hughes decided to purchase twenty-five of these aircraft, projected with four Pratt & Whitney T-34 turboprops, for TWA through his Hughes Tool Company. This was laid down in a purchase agreement signed on Christmas Eve 1954. After a close look at the operating costs calculated by Lockheed for the turboprop ordered by Hughes, TWA managers were shocked. In their opinion, the airline would not make a single dollar of profit with the L-1449! But none of their arguments could change the mind of Howard Hughes. He was determined to buy the L-1449—even against the advice and better arguments of his TWA team.

The ink on the purchase contract was not yet completely dry when Lockheed chief designer Kelly Johnson reported to TWA on January 7, 1955, with bad news: flight tests of the R7V-2 test aircraft had shown that the engine-propeller combination of the T-34 engine did not work. And even worse: there was no economically viable solution to the problems! Only a few weeks after this first alarming news, Pratt & Whitney officially ended the development of the T-34 engine—and the L-1449 project was suddenly without propulsion. Lockheed tried to save what could no longer be saved with the L-1549 model. None of the turboprop alternatives available at the time were really a suitable replacement. The engines were either too large, available too late, or not yet ready for series production.

Parallel studies by TWA and Lockheed showed that the only way forward was to replace the turboprops with conventional Curtiss Wright 3350 EA-2 Turbo Compound piston engines, in combination with large-diameter, slow-turning propellers. Lockheed now named this model L-1649A and prepared an amendment to the purchase agreement signed with TWA in December 1954.

Into this tense situation came the news from Howard Hughes, which had not been discussed with TWA management, that he was demanding a retrofit of the TWA L-1049G fleet with additional Westinghouse J-34 jet engines to increase their cruising speed. Only with difficulty could he be dissuaded by hastily prepared analyses from TWA and Lockheed, neither of which showed any economic benefit. With the jet retrofit of the Super Constellation off the table again, TWA converted the order for twenty-five L-1449s into the identical number of L-1649As by contract amendment of March 29, 1955. The Starliner was thus officially launched, but the now-necessary change in the construction plans also moved the delivery time of the aircraft destined for TWA into 1957 and 1958—and thus ever closer to the imminent jet age on long-haul routes. TWA management was surprised, but also pleased, when Lockheed officially declared the L-1649A project finished in a letter dated April 6, 1955. Obviously, Lockheed had realized that the Starliner had no chance against the faster jets. TWA's management, too, now hoped that, freed from the burden of the unloved propeller plane, it would be able to start into a jet future with the preferred Boeing 707s. But both parties had made this calculation without Howard Hughes. The unpredictable TWA owner insisted that the contract be fulfilled, to the frustration of his own team and the manufacturer—and Lockheed was forced to put the L-1649A into production.

Lockheed managers' worst fears were soon to be realized. Apart from the twenty-five aircraft Lockheed built for TWA, only two other customers, Air France, and Lufthansa, could be found for brand-new L-1649As. In all, only forty-four examples left the final assembly line in Burbank, California. After Lockheed branded its L-1649A as the Starliner at the factory, Air France began operating its aircraft as the Super Starliner, and Lufthansa their new flagship as the Super Star.

IN SERVICE WITH LUFTHANSA

On September 4, 1958, Lufthansa announced the launch of its Senator First Class Service between Germany and New York. Offered exclusively on board its four Super Star aircraft, this was one of the most luxurious ways to cross the North Atlantic in the "Golden Age of Air Travel." The passengers on the Senator premier flight on November 6, 1958, were welcomed on board with a previously unheard-of level of comfort and service—and the Super Star in turn became a flying legend even then. In addition to the extremely comfortable "Comforette" first-class seats, passengers were greeted by an onboard lounge "for chatting, for a game of four, or for a serious business discussion," as a contemporaneous Lufthansa brochure put it. These were the 1950s and thus long before the electronic in-flight entertainment common today found its way into the aircraft. In this bygone "golden" propeller era, conversation with the crew or fellow passengers, culinary delights, and the view out the window of the passing landscape were the only entertainment. Everything on board the Super Star revolved around comfort. In addition to sleeper seats, the aircraft had real beds that could be folded down from the cabin ceiling on night flights. A maximum of thirty-two premium passengers, who were pampered from the first to the last minute of the flight, found space aboard the Lufthansa Senator Service in the Super Star.

This was Lufthansa's luxurious answer to the first jets flown by the British airline BOAC and Pan American, which had entered service a month before the start of the Lufthansa Senator Service and shuttled across the Atlantic much faster than the Super Star. It was not until the 1960 summer timetable that Lufthansa also had a jet model in the form of the Boeing 707-430, which immediately replaced the elegant propeller planes on the prestige route between Frankfurt and New York—and gradually on all other Lufthansa long-haul flights.

Engines and tiptank of a Lufthansa Lockheed L-1049G "Super Constellation."
Courtesy of Lufthansa

BIBLIOGRAPHY

This Douglas R5D, once in service with the US Navy, met the same fate as so many other historic aircraft in the summer of 2013, when the author of this book photographed it in Greybull, Wyoming. *Courtesy of author*

Bjørhovde, Bjørn. *SAS Fly Gjennom Tidene*. Oslo, Norway: DNL/SAS Historielag, 1997.

Davies, R. E.G . *Pan Am: An Airline and Its Aircraft*. Twickenham, UK: Hamlyn, 1987.

Dean, William Patrick. *The ATL-98 Carvair*. Jefferson, NC: McFarland, 2008.

Gieselmann, Heiko, and Katina Treese. *LTU Rückblick, 5 Jahrzente Lebensfreude*. Mühlheim an der Ruhr, Germany: Ok! Communication GmbH, 2005.

Milberry, Larry. *The Canadair North Star*. Toronto: CANAV Books, 1982.

Provan, John. *Big Lift: Die Berliner Luftbruecke*. Bremen, Germany: Edition Temmen, 1998.

Von Vegesack, Alexander, and Jochen Eisenbrand. *Airwold: Design and Architecture for Air Travel*. London: SAGE Publications UK, 2006.

Yenne, Bill. *McDonnell Douglas: A Tale of Two Giants*. Greenwich, CT: Bison Books, 1985.

Contemporaneous documents, Air Canada.
Contemporaneous documents, BOAC.
Contemporaneous documents, Pan Am.
Contemporaneous documents, Scandinavian Airlines.
Contemporaneous documents, Swissair.

ACKNOWLEDGMENTS

CF-KAD was built as a C-54B and operated by Kenting Aviation. It performed ice patrols on behalf of the Canadian federal government. For this purpose, it was equipped with the windshield and canopy of a Canadair Sabre fighter. Photographed at Gander in May 1970. *Courtesy of David Johnston*

Numerous individuals and organizations contributed to the success of this book. I would especially like to thank the following:

John Bezosky, collections manager, Pima Air and Space Museum, US

Ron Handgraaf, ronsaviation shop, the Netherlands

Bernd Keidel, Motorbuch Verlag, Germany

Dave Robinson, www.aviationancestry.co.uk, Great Britain

Tom Weihe and Musante Larsen, Nicolai, Denmark

And my beloved wife, Carol Oxberry, whose continued support through action and advice helped in the making of this book!

Home to KLM and Martin Air Charter (Martinair Holland), the Netherlands was a Douglas four-engined propliner Eldorado. This DC-6A freighter with the registration PH-MAM landed at Copenhagen on April 17, 1968. *Courtesy of Tom Weihe*

The Icelandic airline Loftleidir was a pioneer of low-cost passenger traffic across the North Atlantic. As a nonmember of IATA, the International Air Transport Association, it was able to offer lower ticket prices than the tariff-bound IATA carriers. The "price" the passengers had to pay was an en route stop in Iceland and thus longer flight times compared to other airlines. *Courtesy of Tom Weihe*

The Belgian national carrier Sabena also flew the proven DC-6B on its long-range routes. Traditionally, these were often used on connections to those African states that had previously been Belgian colonies. *Courtesy of Tom Weihe*

This DC-6B of the Danish charter airline Sterling first flew with the registration OY-BAT, starting in 1964, before it received the new Swedish registration SE-ENY on March 19, 1971. The photograph was taken on July 13 of that year, four months after the change of registration from Denmark to Sweden. *Courtesy of Tom Weihe*

THE AUTHOR
WOLFGANG BORGMANN

Wolfgang Borgmann's enthusiasm for aviation was passed on to him by his parents, who were active in the aviation field. In his early years, he began building up an aviation historical collection that provides numerous rare photos and documents, as well as exciting background information, for his books. Since 1995, Borgmann has been active as an aviation journalist and since 2008 as an author. He lives in Oerlinghausen, Germany. His website is www.aerojournalist.de.